SURE-HIRE RÉSUMÉS

SURE-HIRE RÉSUMÉS

Robbie Miller Kaplan

amacom

American Management Association

Library of Congress Cataloging-in Publication Data

Kaplan, Robbie Miller.
    Sure-hire resumés / Robbie Miller Kaplan.
        p.   cm.
    Updated ed. of: Résumés. c1987.
    Includes bibliographical references.
    ISBN 0-8144-7728-3
      1. Résumés (Employment) I. Kaplan, Robbie Miller. Résumés.
II. Title.
HF5383.K37 1989   89-81023
808'.06665—dc20   CIP

The first edition was originally published as *Resumes: The Write Stuff*
by Garrett Park Press.

Printing number

10 9 8 7 6 5 4 3 2 1

Lovingly
Dedicated
to My Husband,
Jim

Contents

Preface

You may be asking yourself, "Why should I buy this résumé book?" Because it works, that's why.

I have worked with thousands of job seekers since I first wrote *Résumés: The Write Stuff*. Despite all the résumé books on the market, many people *still* find résumé writing a difficult and frustrating task. To make the job easier and more efficient, I have written this new edition—a totally updated and expanded version of my original book. You will find twice as many résumés in the makeover section covering twice as many professions—all management-level careers. I have experimented with new formats and I'm excited with the results. You will be too. Just like any other task, writing a résumé requires skills, and this book will teach you those skills.

Writing your résumé is the first step to take when you are considering a job change. It is an opportunity to assess your qualifications and target your search. The first chapter will assist you by providing a step-by-step approach to recording your past experiences, discovering your accomplishments, and assessing their importance to your overall career plan.

Exciting technological advances make career assistance software an alternative way for you to produce a quality résumé. I have evaluated three major software programs and reproduce the sample résumés I created using each of them. The comparative information provided about each program will help you choose the program that works best for you.

A unique résumé section highlights the errors and suggests improvements in 25 original résumés and presents a revised version for each of them. Additional information, tools, and the most current resources and technology are provided to guide you through the actual writing.

Since cover letters are a very important part of the job search, I went right to the experts—top personnel managers in major institutions and corporations. I asked them what kind of cover letter caught their attention and they responded by actually writing sample cover letters themselves.

Looking for a job can be exciting. Planning a job search and having a sense of control wards off some of the feelings of rejection that are inevitable in a job hunt. Knowing that you are presenting your qualifications in the most favorable light will give you confidence throughout your job campaign.

Wherever you are in your career—changing jobs or seeking a promotion—this book provides you with all the information you'll need to prepare a résumé and cover letter that will work.

Follow the guidelines and you will get results! Good luck and good reading.

R. M. K.

Acknowledgments

M^{any} thanks:

- To Gail Crockett, Mary Beth McCormac, Bert Holtje, Mark Dorio, Andrea Pedolsky, Bob Calvert, and Mary Fairchild for your resources and support
- To Jim Kaplan for your invaluable technical assistance, patience, and support
- To Wade Robinson and Unisys Corporation, Debbie Pivnick and Xerox Canada, Gerald Albright and BASF Corporation, James Herger and COMSAT Corporation, William Lockom and Beth Israel Hospital, Brenda Watson and the *New York Times*, Jack Phillips and Secor Bank, and John Barrett and the Boston Public Library for your time and contribution
- To my mother for all of your assistance and support
- To Ileene and Gary Hoffman for all of your help, but most important, for your friendship and encouragement

1 To Include or Not to Include? That Is the Question

What Is a Résumé?

A résumé is not an autobiography, nor is it a chronicle of all of your experiences. It should summarize experiences relevant to your career goals, highlight your accomplishments, and show what you learned from those experiences.

The résumé is a marketing tool. It should sell you to prospective employers the same way an advertisement entices you to purchase a product. It is the first impression employers will have of you, and from it they will decide if they want to meet you.

There is no right or wrong way to write a résumé—only a better way. Your résumé should be as individual as you are and needs to be designed so it will express your unique qualities. Copying a canned résumé format will not work, because it probably won't highlight your skills and abilities to your advantage.

Writing a résumé is a good self-assessment. It is an opportunity to focus on your strengths and interests and will help you prepare for a job interview.

The format of your résumé should be carefully considered and developed. Ask yourself, "How will this information look best? What qualifications are most important for this career area?"

Résumés don't get jobs, but résumés can open or close the door to job opportunities. The goal of your résumé is to make the employer want to talk with you—to make you one of the select group to whom job interviews are offered.

A résumé should not be set in stone. As you gain new experiences, develop different career goals, or advance to higher levels of work, you will draft different résumés. The basic principles remain the same and the techniques highlighted in this book should help you throughout your working career.

Types of Résumés

The two basic types of résumés are chronological and functional.

The *chronological résumé* is the traditional résumé. It is a summary of your education and experience beginning with the most recent and working backwards in time. See the résumé of Michael K. James for an example. This form works best for an individual who

1

MICHAEL K. JAMES

4300 Plantation Boulevard, Syracuse, New York 13610 (716) 764-3325

OBJECTIVE   A challenging career opportunity in public accounting which will provide growth potential leading to partnership status.

EDUCATION

1989   **M.S.**, Syracuse University, Syracuse, New York

Major: Accounting (GPA accounting courses - 3.6)

1981   **B.S.**, The American University, Washington, D.C.

Major: Business Administration

**PROFESSIONAL
EXPERIENCE**

1985 - Present   **Senior Auditor**, Onondaga Management Inc., Syracuse, New York

Analyze G/L accounts and prepare working paper schedules in compliance with independent auditor specifications. Audit payroll, daily cash receipts, and prepare unaudited financial statements.

1983 - 1985   **Assistant Controller**, Universal Carpet Mills, Liverpool, New York

Accounting and administrative responsibility for a vertically integrated organization with sales of $60 million. Prepared budgets and financial statements, analyzed payables and receivables and implemented credit and collection programs. Prepared and audited employee and sub-contractor payroll, state sales taxes, and bank reconciliations. Planned and controlled physical inventory and year end audit.

Direct responsibility for a staff of six; recruited, supervised, provided training and development, implemented changes in personnel policy, and appraised performance.

1982 - 1983   **Credit Control Manager**, Parkview-Gem Inc., Syracuse, New York

Accountable for all store funds. Determined credit worthiness of revolving and time payment customers. Developed and implemented internal control procedures to obtain maximum efficiency in expense and inventory control. Minimized exposure to uncollectible accounts by establishing credit policies and control procedures.

1981 - 1982   **Assistant Credit Control Manager,** Parkview-Gem Inc., Tysons Corner, Virginia

Entry level position which included training in credit analysis and control procedures. Prepared daily reports for store and corporate management. Supervised and coordinated scheduling for credit staff and cashier.

1981 -1987   **Tax Consultant and Preparer**, H&R Block, Virginia and New York

Prepared individual and small unincorporated business tax returns.

has followed a specific career plan with jobs of increased responsibility. Some employers will only accept chronological résumés.

The chronological résumé does not work well for an individual with frequent job changes, gaps in employment history, or someone who wishes to use skills acquired in non-work settings, such as volunteer activities, to emphasize qualifications for employment.

The *functional résumé* highlights your skills, experience, and accomplishments in specific areas such as administration, communications, marketing, management, or planning. It may or may not include a work history. Harriet Hoachum's résumé is an example of a functional résumé.

In the past, personnel managers felt individuals were hiding something when they used a functional résumé. In recent years, it has become an accepted form and can be very effective for:

- Individuals who are reentering after a work gap
- Those who have or will be changing careers
- Individuals who have been in the same or similar positions for a long period and the work responsibilities are repetitive when listed chronologically.

The Essentials

It is important that all of the following information is included in your résumé:

1. *Name, complete mailing address, and phone number, including area code.* If possible, also include your business number. The more accessible you are, the more likely you will be reached.
2. A *Career Objective* that indicates the kind of job you are seeking. It should be specific enough to imply that you know what you are looking for, but not so specific that you won't be considered for a broader range of positions. A career objective should give you a sense of direction. It defines your job target so that you can choose appropriate experiences to support the objective. Avoid pronouns. They make an objective sound self-serving. Employers want to know what you can do for them, not what they can do for you. If you feel that a career objective will limit your job opportunities, you can use a summary (discussed in The Optionals).
3. *Education.*

   - If high school is your last graduation, include that.
   - If you graduated from a college or technical school, no further.
   - If you have an associate's degree and a bachelor's, include both.

HARRIET HOACHUM
34 Dole Drive, Honolulu, Hawaii 96822
(808) 444-1900

CAREER OBJECTIVE: A position in personnel management.

EXPERIENCE

Personnel

Administered benefits program: medical, dental, long term disability, and life insurance. Ensured compliance with workman's compensation; prepared and submitted reports as requested by Federal and State governments.

Prepared and administered orientation program for new employees; maintained and administered programs for promotions, reviews, salary increases, and profit sharing; coordinated recruiting and advertised job openings.

Training

Develop curriculum and teach personal computer applications on government awarded contracts. Train on-site and in workshops.

Write reference materials, prepare layout and graphics, order materials, arrange publication, proof material, and distribute manuals.

Trained supervisors and employees in word processing, electronic spreadsheets(Multiplan), system administration and management, and introductory and advanced operations.

EMPLOYMENT HISTORY

Creative Systems, Honolulu, Hawaii
System Analyst/Trainer, 1986 - present
Trainers, Inc., Honolulu, Hawaii
Education Specialist, 1984 - 1986
Assistant to the Director of Personnel, 1983 - 1984
University of Hawaii, Honolulu, Hawaii
Research Specialist, 1979 - 1983
International Tourist Association, Honolulu, Hawaii
Administrative Assistant, 1973 - 1976

University of Hawaii, Honolulu, Hawaii
Bachelor of Science, 1961
Professional Development
"Unix", "Train the Trainer", "Effective Proposal Writing"

- If you have associate's, bachelor's, and master's degrees, include the bachelor's and master's only.
- If you have a Ph.D., include your bachelor's and master's degrees and Ph.D., but go back no further.
- Include location of school (city and state), title of major field or fields, subject of any major research, date of graduation or completion, academic honors (if any), or major activities while in school.

4. *Employer-related training and additional courses.* Attendance at formal courses or on-the-job training received in current or past employment.
5. *Work experience or history*, including skills and accomplishments. As important as what you did is how well you performed, so emphasize your unique accomplishments.
6. *Professional associations and memberships.*
7. *Professional licenses, honors, publications, and certifications.*
8. *Specific skills* that you have such as typing, shorthand, and language fluency. Stress those related to your career goal. It may not help to stress scuba-diving skills if you are interested in a technical research position.

The Optionals

The following are areas you might want to consider. Beware of wasting space. Choose only those areas that will enhance your qualifications.

1. *Personal data.* It is illegal for an employer to ask about your age, marital status, and children. Why offer any information that would give someone the opportunity to discriminate against you? It is in your best interest to offer information on your résumé that shows you to be the most qualified candidate. For all information you plan to include, ask yourself, "Does this information make me a better candidate?" If not, don't include it. Have you ever heard of anyone writing "Health: Poor"? Use every bit of available space to market yourself.
2. *Hobbies and interests.* Unless you have had unusual accomplishments in hobbies and interests, don't include them. Save this information for the application or the interview. *Do* use this area if a hobby or interest shows great accomplishment or can be tied into the position you are seeking.
3. *References.* At the time of the job interview, you will be asked for the names of your references, so why waste a line of space that reads "References Furnished Upon Request" when you can use the space to market yourself? I always suggest elimi-

nating this line on your résumé. Many experts disagree. But everyone agrees that it doesn't make sense to waste valuable space by listing names, titles, addresses, and phone numbers of people prepared to comment on your qualifications. Besides using valuable space, you run the risk that too many prospective employers will call your references. If you abuse your references, you may lose them. Use them only for positions you are really interested in obtaining. Be sure to contact your references ahead of time to discuss positions of interest. It is helpful to send them a copy of your résumé to reinforce your skills and accomplishments. This may assist them in responding to inquiries.

4. *Summary.* A summary is used as a capsule of experience. It gets the message across. Use it for extensive work experience or to highlight a particular skill or area of interest. Some individuals prefer to use a summary instead of a career objective. The summary can be called: Career History, Career Highlights, Summary of Experience, Qualifications Summary, or Career Summary.

A summary works well for:

- Persons with ten or more years of experience. A few opening sentences show a wide variety of experience and accomplishments.
- Individuals who have changed careers. A résumé might not flow smoothly and a summary states up front what you want an employer to know.
- Those with experience in both the public and private sector. The summary will pull it all together.

Isn't There a Law Against That?

Laws were created to protect you from discrimination. Do not include any information on your résumé that would give an employer the opportunity to discriminate against you. The Civil Rights Act of 1964 prohibits discrimination on the basis of color, race, sex, religion, or national origin in employment decisions by employers, employment agencies, and labor organizations who have 15 or more employees. A 1972 amendment brought the federal government under the Act and prohibits discrimination against individuals because of pregnancy, childbirth, or related medical conditions.

The Age Discrimination in Employment Act, passed in 1967 and amended in 1979, protects individuals over age 40 up to age 70 against discrimination based on age. Employers who have 12 or more employees are affected.

Handicapped persons are protected under the Rehabilitation Act of 1973, if they are able to perform the job. Only companies that get federal money are affected.

Useful Sources of Information

It is hard to remember all the job information you will need to outline your experience. Go through your records and look for:

1. Job advertisements . . . yours or similar ones
2. Job descriptions
3. Standards of performance
4. Performance evaluations
5. Offer letters
6. Letters of commendation
7. Certificates of completion

Great Beginnings

There is an old Chinese proverb that says, "A long journey begins with but a single step." Often the hardest part of developing the résumé is to take that first step. It is easier if you can organize your efforts by following the steps listed below.

Step 1

Sit down and chronologically list all of your work experience—paid and unpaid. Consider fraternal, military, community, religious, and educational experiences. See the list of sources of information for the experiences.

Even if you have extensive paid experience, list your unpaid experience as well. Most people use skills and abilities they really enjoy in their volunteer activities. In outlining these experiences, you may see a trend that you can translate into related experiences helpful in your job hunt.

For example:

Work Experience

1984–present	American Medical Association	Personnel Recruiter
1982–1984	American Medical Association	Personnel Assistant
1983–1984	Valley Community Library	Volunteer Coordinator
1981–present	United Church	Newsletter Editor
1979–1982	Valley Community Hospital	Personnel Assistant

1976–1979	Valley Community Hospital	Personnel Secretary
1974–1977	Valley Community Hospital	Gift Shop Aide
1970–1976	Jones, Williams, Inc.	Secretary
1968–1970	Davis Community College	Yearbook Staff

Step 2

Once you have listed all of your work experience in order, take a separate sheet of paper for each experience and develop a complete list of responsibilities.

For example:

Personnel Recruiter Responsibilities

1. Recruit staff.
2. Serve as Affirmative Action Coordinator.
3. Serve as College Campus Representative.
4. Administer appropriate employment tests.
5. Develop and update orientation program.
6. Give orientation presentations.
7. Maintain thorough familiarity with organizational structure and personnel policies to present to prospective employees.
8. Act as liaison with the community.

Step 3

Take separate sheets of paper for each area of responsibility. List all the tasks required to carry out that responsibility. For example:

Responsibility: Recruit Staff

Tasks

1. Research local publications to select the most appropriate for placing classified ads.
2. Write ads for classifieds.
3. Place ads in publications.
4. Work with local college placement offices to list job openings.
5. Screen potential candidates on phone.
6. Set up interviews.
7. Interview candidates.
8. Check references.
9. Evaluate skills and merits of each set of top five candidates.

10. Rank the top five candidates.
11. Make job offers.

Step 4

It is important to show both responsibilities and accomplishments. To do this, review your tasks and look at the problems, challenges, and obstacles that you have had to overcome. What actions did you take to successfully complete your tasks? What did you accomplish?

For example:

Responsibility: Recruit Staff

Problem

1. Fill entry-level management positions with individuals who will remain in position and be interested in career advancement.
2. Hire candidates who will be a good match to reduce turnover.

Actions Taken

1. Researched periodicals to attract most appropriate candidates.
2. Worked with local colleges.
3. Offered and gave several free speeches on job-hunting techniques to get our organization's name out to the public.

Accomplishments

Reduced turnover by 20 percent through attracting, interviewing, and carefully screening a large base of qualified candidates.

Step 5

Outline your education chronologically. Include colleges, technical or professional schools, and business or professional training. Include programs completed and those in progress. List everything. You will later eliminate those that will not support your career objective.

For example:

Education

1986	Management Skills, American Medical Association
1985	Effective Business Communication, American Medical Association
1984	Management Studies, American Medical Association
1983	Effective Time Management, Adult Education

1981	Bachelor of Science in Business Administration, Ohio State University
1979	Personnel Procedures, Valley Community Hospital
1974	Secretarial Procedures, Valley Community Hospital
1970	Associate in Applied Arts, Davis Community College
1970	Effective Listening Techniques, Adult Education
1970	Speed Writing, Adult Education

The Elements, Dear Watson

The astute Sherlock Holmes and the bumbling Dr. Watson combined their talents to solve hundreds of fictional mysteries. They used a variety of research tools to outwit criminals. You need to assemble effective tools to outwit those job seekers competing with you for openings.

Tools

The essential tools are a dictionary and thesaurus. A synonym dictionary is very helpful as well. They will assist you in checking spelling and eliminating redundancy.

A handbook for grammar and punctuation is an asset. Resources are listed below. Check your library or local bookstore for additional sources.

DEVLIN, JOSEPH. *A Dictionary of Synonyms and Antonyms.* New York: Warner Books, 1983.

The Merriam-Webster Dictionary. New York: Pocket Books, 1974.

QUINN, MICHELLE. *Katharine Gibbs Handbook of Business English.* New York: Macmillan Publishing Company, 1982.

RODALE, J. I. *The Synonym Finder.* New York: Warner Books, 1978.

ROGET, PETER MARK. *Roget's Thesaurus of English Words and Phrases.* New York: Chatham River Press, 1979.

STRUNK, WILLIAM, JR., and WHITE, E. B. *The Elements of Style.* New York: Macmillan Publishing Co., 1979.

Punctuation

Different elements of punctuation simplify reading and understanding. It is critically important that the reader find your résumé easy to follow. Your goal is to develop a résumé that will visibly highlight your most marketable skills. Proper punctuation plays an important part in the presentation of your résumé.

A **semi-colon (;)** is used to separate parts of equal significance:

1. In a series when the items in the series already contain commas.

Managed office staff of five. Hired, supervised, dismissed; ordered supplies, controlled inventory, issued purchase orders; acted as manager during owner's absence.

2. Between two or more independent clauses when they are not connected by a coordinate conjunction (coordinate conjunctions are *and, or, but,* and *nor*).

Developed a new program for typing skills; enrollment increased by 20%.
   Employment dates are listed first; names of organizations and job titles are listed second.

A **hyphen (-)** is found within words. There are so many rules for hyphenation that you should consult a dictionary or grammar book for correct spelling.

part-time	two-thirds
long-range	all-out effort
up-to-date	on-the-job training
past-due account	

A **colon (:)** is used to alert readers that an explanation, list, enumeration, or quotation will follow.

Management responsibilities include: recruiting, supervising, reviewing performance, counseling, and dismissing.

Use the colon after the salutation in a business letter.

Dear Mr. Madison:

A **comma (,)** alerts the reader to a brief pause.
Use a comma:

1. In a series of three or more words, phrases, or dependent clauses. Use between each of the items and before the coordinate conjunction that separates the last two. The comma before the coordinate conjunction is required in business writing.

Design, lay out, and proof graphic arts for newsletter.

2. Between the individual elements in addresses and names of places.

12 Hollywood Avenue, Tuckahoe, New York 10707
Spanish internship in Madrid, Spain

Active Verbs

administer	counsel	integrate	procure
advise	create	interview	produce
analyze	delegate	introduce	propose
anticipate	demonstrate	invent	provide
appraise	design	inventory	recommend
arrange	determine	investigate	reconcile
assess	develop	launch	record
assign	devise	lead	recruit
assist	direct	locate	represent
audit	distribute	maintain	research
brief	document	manage	resolve
budget	draft	mediate	review
calculate	edit	monitor	schedule
check	establish	negotiate	solve
classify	evaluate	operate	substantiate
coach	execute	order	supervise
collect	formulate	organize	teach
communicate	identify	originate	test
compile	implement	participate	track
compose	inform	perform	train
conceive	initiate	plan	update
conduct	inspect	prepare	utilize
consult	install	present	validate
control	institute	prioritize	verify
coordinate	instruct	process	write

Active Voice Verbs and Wordiness

When choosing verbs, use verbs that are in the active voice. See the list of active voice verbs used in business. The term *voice* refers to whether the subject of the sentence performs the action or receives it. When a subject performs the action, it is in the active voice and appears in the first part of the sentence. When the subject receives the action, it is in the passive voice and appears in the last part of the sentence. Also, avoid using unnecessary words that slow down your writing. Active sentences are concise. The following demonstrates how you can frequently reword sentences to replace passive voice verbs with active ones and to tighten wordy phrases by using active verbs:

Passive: Transportation routings were developed for various classes of mail.
Active: Developed transportation routings for various classes of mail.
Passive: New personnel were classified.
Active: Classified new personnel.
Wordy: Responsible for management of personnel office.
Active: Managed personnel office.

Wordy:	Provide management, guidance, and direction to staff of five.
Active:	Manage, guide, and direct staff of five.
Wordy:	In charge of scheduling 100 police officers.
Active:	Schedule 100 police officers.

Characteristics of Active Voice

1. Forceful and direct
2. Less wordy
3. Authoritative
4. Easier to understand

What Do I Do Now?

You now have a written history of your experience and education. It is time to decide whether a chronological or a functional résumé will highlight and market your skills and accomplishments.

Holly Wallach has six years of experience with two brokerage firms. She has been promoted three times. She plans on pursuing a management position with another brokerage firm. The chronological résumé would work well for her.

Donna Webster has been a homemaker for 12 years. She has coordinated fund raising and publicity for the Red Cross and Parent Teacher Association. Donna would like to begin full-time work as a fund-raising manager or public relations coordinator. A functional résumé emphasizing her skills, projects, and performance would work best.

Henry Allen is retired. He would like to do some part-time work. He is financially secure and would like a position that ties in with his love of stamp collecting. A functional résumé would draw attention to his different collections, exhibits he has created, conferences attended, articles written and published in newsletters, and association memberships.

Once you have decided on the type of résumé you will use, review your working papers and choose the information that best describes what you have done and what you have to offer. Most people discover they have more marketable skills than they realized. All of these will probably not go into your résumé. Select information that best supports your career objective. Concentrate on clarity. Beware of writing a job description. It's not what the employer can do for you, but what you can do for the employer.

Piecing the Puzzle

The format of your résumé is the way you organize information. The structure you choose should highlight your unique achievements and

---

Format Checklist

☐ Do you have highly marketable skills such as word processing, accounting, or computer programming? You might emphasize these at the top of the résumé under "Skills."

☐ Do you have unusual or prized work history or experience? You might want to include a short "Work History" at the beginning. This can be used when a Career Objective is also present.

☐ Are you a recent graduate? Do your studies qualify you for a new career field, one in which you don't have many years of previous work experience? You might want to begin your résumé with "Education."

☐ Do you have a great deal of experience in your field or skills and accomplishments that qualify you for the position you seek? You may want to begin your résumé with "Experience."

---

traits, whether they involve education, skills, or experience. A résumé format is as individual as you are and should reflect your personal strengths. Are you a winner? Toot your own horn. If you don't, no one else will. Play up your achievements. Stress your strong points and downplay or omit your weaknesses. The accompanying checklist will help you decide on a format.

Will your résumé stand out from the competition? Most hiring personnel will scan a résumé rather than read it. They will scan from top to bottom. Ask yourself, "Which areas most qualify me for the positions I seek?" List these categories first.

All résumés should begin with name, address, phone number, and career objective or summary. Build your résumé to support the objective by adding information that reinforces and strengthens your objective. The rest of the résumé can be structured at your discretion. Most individuals center their name, address, and phone number. I would encourage you to be creative. There are numberous examples of different formats and layouts in the second chapter of this book. Most résumés tend to look the same—make yours eye-catching. *Caution:* Don't be so creative or unusual that your résumé stands out too much. You want it to be regarded with interest, not amusement.

The Final Product

There are many choices for résumé production. You can use a typewriter, word processor, word processing or résumé software, desktop publishing software, or a typesetter. Look for cost, quality, and availability when deciding how to present your finished résumé. The following information will help you decide.

Type or Typeset

Your résumé will probably be reorganized and retyped at least five times before you are satisfied with the final product. You might decide to make more changes once you begin interviewing. If at all possible, have your résumé in a format that can easily be changed and updated. Word processors, word processing and résumé software, and desktop publishing offer ease in editing and modifying a résumé. A résumé done on a typewriter or by a typesetter can't be changed without starting over from scratch.

There are many business services available for résumé production. Locate these through the classified section of your newspaper or the yellow pages of your phone directory. Find out what type of equipment is used and the cost. Ask to see samples of completed résumés as fonts and elements vary. Some look great, others mediocre. Be a smart shopper. Understand the services that you are contracting for.

If you have access to a personal computer, it is easier than ever to create a résumé yourself. Résumé and word processing software are available in a wide range of pricing. You will need a printer to produce your résumé. The software documentation will specify what printers are compatible with the software. Laser printers produce the highest-quality product at the highest price. The 24-pin dot-matrix printers are practical, economical, and letter quality. Don't use any printer that is not letter quality as it will detract from the résumé's appearance. Check your local printers for laser printing services.

Computer Software

To help you select a software program for producing your résumé, I experimented with three software packages: WordPerfect, The Resume Kit, and Re$ume!. I chose WordPerfect because it's the best-selling word processing program among PC users. The Resume Kit and Re$ume! are two programs widely available in most retail stores.

The résumé software allows you to input your résumé data and will then format and actually produce a résumé for you. You'll get the best results, however, if you write and choose a format for your résumé prior to inputting it. Since WordPerfect is primarily a word processing package, you will have to write and format your résumé before running the program.

Examples of the same résumé produced on each of the three software programs follow. You will be able to evaluate the programs and your needs with information that includes documentation, ease of use, features, additional features, tips, disadvantages, system requirements, and the mailing address of each software company.

WordPerfect

This is the most widely used word processing package for the IBM PC and is considered to be the industry standard. You have to write your résumé and format it before beginning the program.

Documentation: Good. Documentation is for the entire word processing system. Cue card on the computer assists you while you use the program.

Ease of use: You will need to learn how to use WordPerfect before beginning a résumé. A five- to seven-hour introductory course will enable you to input, edit, and print a résumé.

Features: Bold, underline, uppercase, lines, columns, indentations, justification, centering, box text, spell check, and thesaurus. Comes with a lifetime toll-free support system and Laserjet support.

Additional features: Additional fonts available for use with Laserjet.

Tips: To fit properly on the page, center page top to bottom (use Page Format, Shift F8, #2, #1). Use Indent (F4) rather than Tab because Indent does an automatic wrap. To right-hand justify indentations at the beginning of the indented material, use Page Format, Shift F8, #1, #3 justification on; at the end, use Page Format, Shift F8, #1, #3 justification off. You will need to do this for every indented paragraph. When using underline, end it after each word unless you want a continuous underline.

Disadvantages: This a word processing program and it offers no assistance in writing and producing a résumé.

System requirements: IBM PS/2, PC, or compatible. DOS 2.1 or higher. 384K of memory. Two disk drives, hard disk recommended. Use CGA, EGA, VGA, or Hercules for viewing graphics. Printer necessary for printing résumé and cover letters.

For information: WordPerfect Corporation, 1555 N. Technology Way, Orem, UT 84057

HELEN CLARK
55 Maple Lane
Denver, Colorado 80203
(303) 766-9321

SUMMARY OF QUALIFICATIONS

A service-oriented manager, able to establish and maintain effective agency operations. Strong technical skills, with a thorough working knowledge of airline systems and Sabre.

CAREER OBJECTIVE: A management position with a commercial travel agency.

EDUCATION: A. S., Travel and Tourism, 1981
Collins Community College, Chicago, Illinois

EXPERIENCE: **AMERICAN EXPRESS,** Denver, Colorado
Assistant Manager
1985 - present

Assist in management of agency with a staff of ten specializing in international travel. Train new agents, develop and implement office procedures, and manage staff in supervisor's absence.

Initiated and implemented a customer relations program. Created advertising and direct mail campaign resulting in $50,000 in new business.

CHASE WORLD TRAVEL, Denver, Colorado
Travel Agent
1983 - 1985

Handled international travel arrangements for individuals and groups. Prepared itineraries and arranged reservations for airline, accommodations, and car rentals. Provided information on geography, required papers, and currency exchanges.

UNITED AIRLINES, Chicago, Illinois
Reservation Agent
1981 - 1983

Assisted customers in making reservations for domestic and international travel. Handled phone inquiries on fares, schedules, and arrival/departure updates. Offered information on routes, time schedules, rates, and types of accommodations.

SKILLS: Fluent in French and Spanish, Sabre trained.

The Resume Kit

A résumé software program for the IBM PC. Works best if you write your résumé and format it before working with the program.

Documentation: Excellent. The user's manual guides you through the program as well as providing effective information on how to write a résumé and look for a job.

Ease of use: Fairly easy to use. Documentation takes you through the program. The program has an easy-to-understand help feature and drop-down menus.

Features: Automatic formatting—choose from nine résumé formats; spell check (with 100,000 words) for each screen; custom feature that allows you to change font, layout, margins, and indentations. Context-sensitive help feature and résumé writing tips are always available by pressing function keys.

Additional features: Calls itself a "complete job search assistant." Offers letter writing with a built-in word processor, mail merge, and built-in calendar for appointment schedule. It has a 30-day warranty and free four-month employment listing of résumés on the worldwide career advancement network through on-line services of International Business Network. There is in-house service for laser printing résumés.

Tips: Read and follow your user's manual carefully.

Disadvantages: There are a set number of character spaces for the experience section. There isn't enough room to add all of the accomplishments in the sample résumé.

System requirements: IBM PS/2, PC, or compatible. DOS 2.0 or higher. 384K of memory. One or two floppy disk drives. Hard disk is optional. Graphics adapter for on-screen preview. Printer necessary for printing résumés and cover letters.

For information: Spinnaker Software, 1 Kendall Square, Cambridge, MA 02139

HELEN CLARK
55 Maple Lane
Denver, Colorado 80203
(303) 766-9321

GENERAL SUMMARY	A service-oriented manager, able to establish and maintain effective agency operations. Strong technical skills, with a thorough working knowledge of airline systems and Sabre.

CAREER OBJECTIVE

A management position with a commercial travel agency.

EDUCATION

Collins Community College, Chicago, Illinois
A. S. in Travel and Tourism, 1981

BUSINESS EXPERIENCE

AMERICAN EXPRESS, Denver, Colorado
Assistant Manager   1985 to present
Assist in management of agency with a staff of ten specializing in international travel. Train new agents, develop and implement office procedures, and manage staff in supervisor's absence. Initiated and implemented customer relations program.

CHASE WORLD TRAVEL, Denver, Colorado
Travel Agent   1983 to 1985
Handled international travel arrangements for individuals and groups. Prepared itineraries and arranged reservations for airline, accommodations, and car rentals. Provided information on geography, required papers, and currency exchanges.

UNITED AIRLINES, Chicago, Illinois
Reservation Agent   1981 to 1983
Assisted customers in making reservations for domestic and international travel. Handled phone inquiries on fares, schedules, and arrival/departure updates. Offered information on routes, time schedules, rates, and types of accommodations.

SKILLS

Fluent in French and Spanish; Sabre trained.

Re$ume!

A menu-based résumé software program for the IBM PC. Works best if you write your résumé and format it before beginning program.

Documentation: Fair. You must print a 30-page user's guide off the disk.

Ease of use: Not the easiest program to use. It is sometimes difficult to figure out how to fix a problem. You must complete all fields in some areas for the section to pick up (for example, education would not initially print on the sample résumé, because the skill section was not completed under "Post High School Education").

Features: Offers three formats: chronological, accomplished, and targeted. You can enter up to six past positions. It includes a "Skills Catalog" with 300 prelisted skills and has the ability to add specialized skills. The program utilizes a data base from which it searches skills words, automatically updates, and performs mathematical calculations. You can change the layout order. It has a separate screen for each work experience in which you can list three accomplishments.

Additional features: Not copy protected. Two printing choices: Print directly or capture formatted disk as an ASCII file. Load ASCII file into a word processor and add additional "embellishments." A professional version is available for résumé preparers, educators, training instructors, and employment counselors.

Tips: Read and follow your user's manual carefully.

Disadvantages: Although it claims that it writes your résumé, you still need to know how to write a résumé for this program to be effective. The user guide does not provide information and you will need another résumé writing source. The career summary it provides and calculates is not well written. Without embellishments, it does not look great visually.

Systems requirements: IBM PS/2, PC, or compatible. DOS 2.0 or higher. 192K of memory. One or two floppy disk drives. Hard disk optional. Printer necessary for printing résumé.

For information: North American InfoNet., P.O. Box 750008, Petaluma, CA 94975

HELEN CLARK
55 MAPLE LANE
DENVER, CO 80203
Home: (303) 766-9321

CAREER OBJECTIVE:

A management position with a commercial travel agency.

SUMMARY:

More than 3 years of experience in SERVICE-ORIENTED, AIRLINE
SYSTEMS and SABRE including supervision.

EDUCATION:

1981 A.S. Collins Community College   Travel and Tourism

EXPERIENCE:

1985-Present: Assistant Manager
AMERICAN EXPRESS,
Denver, CO
Assist in management of agency with a staff of ten
specializing in international travel. Train new agents,
develop and implement office procedures, and manage staff
in supervisor's absence.

1983-1985: Travel Agent
CHASE WORLD TRAVEL,
Denver, CO
Handled international travel arrangements for individuals
and groups. Prepared itineraries and arranged reservations for airline, accommodations, and car rentals. Provided information on geography, required papers, and
currency exchanges.

1981-1983: Reservation Agent
UNITED AIRLINES,
Chicago, IL
Assisted customers in making reservations for domestic
and international travel. Handled phone inquiries on
fares, schedules, and arrival/departure updates. Offered
information on routes, time schedules, rates, and types
of accommodations.

Copy or Print

Most résumés are copied rather than printed. If a good-quality copier is used, the finished product can be excellent. Check prices with your printer to determine which is your best alternative.

Résumés can be copied on individual copiers or copied and printed at local print shops. When copying yourself, ensure that the machine has proper toner and developer and that you have cleaned the platen glass so that the copies will be clear.

Résumés can also be run off individually from a word processor or computer printer so that each résumé will look like an original. Check with your local printing shop and word-processing service to compare costs.

Paper

Résumés and cover letters are most effective when done on the same quality paper. There are a number of options for paper selection.

Your local stationery supply store will stock 8½″ × 11″ bond paper in buff, cream, white, and pale gray colors with matching envelopes. These are good color choices. Your résumé can be copied or printed on this paper and additional paper purchased for cover letters. The approximate cost for 80 sheets and 50 envelopes is under $15.

Your local print shop will often stock the quality paper needed to copy or print your résumé. Additional paper can be purchased for cover letters.

Another alternative is ordering personal business stationery, 8½″ × 11″ matching second sheets, and envelopes. Format your résumé so that it can be copied or printed right on the letterhead. Use the second sheet for a second page, if needed. This choice can look extremely professional and effective. The approximate cost for 250 printed letterhead and envelopes is $125.

Fifteen Tips

1. A résumé should fit on one or two pages. If you have extensive work experience, it is fine to use two. If you are a recent graduate, one is considered best. I have reviewed résumés that were seven pages long when I was desperate to fill a position, but the competition is too fierce to chance a lengthy résumé. *Never* use a two-sided copier.

2. A two-page résumé should always be stapled together. You do not need to number or type your name on the second page as the staple will hold them together. Do not put your

résumé in a folder or plastic insert as it may need to be copied and distributed.

3. The tenses should all agree. The objective should be in the present tense, present experiences in the present tense, and past experiences in the past tense. Do not shift tense.

4. If you have accomplishments in your present position that are in the past tense, you may want to include this information a few spaces below your current experience. This will emphasize the accomplishment and not cause a shift in tense. If you have past and present information for a functional résumé, begin skill areas with the present information and follow with the past.

5. Quantify whenever possible. It makes a difference whether you managed a staff of 2 or a staff of 12. Follow basic guidelines when using numbers; spell out numbers from one to ten and write figures from 11 upwards. Numbers of the same category should be treated alike throughout a paragraph (see staffs of 2 and 12 above); do not use figures for some and spell out others. When a number follows a dollar sign ($), always write figures (for example: $5 million).

6. Use the same grammatical form for related points. For example:

> **Wrong:** Development of curriculum, co-lead groups, evaluate program compliance, and writing grant proposals.
>
> **Right:** Developing curriculum, co-leading groups, evaluating program compliance, and writing grant proposals.

7. A dictionary should never leave your side. Many recruiters toss out every résumé with a misspelled word or typo, viewing this as carelessness and a lack of interest. Always proofread for errors and check your spelling. Some culprits are hypenated words whose meanings are changed without the hyphen. I was once embarrassed during a presentation by writing *resign* when I should have used *re-sign*.

8. Edit your résumé many times to improve word choice and eliminate redundancy. Give a copy of your résumé to a trusted friend to proof and highlight the redundancies. Use a synonym dictionary, a dictionary, and a thesaurus.

9. Avoid using jargon, acronyms, and abbreviations. You want your reader to understand what you have to say. I prefer degrees to be written out, but this is a personal choice and they can be abbreviated. Certain degrees should be abbreviated, such as: M.D., J.D., Ph.D., and D.D.S. Be consistent. Either spell out or abbreviate all degrees.

10. Don't use flashy colors, unusual, or odd-sized paper. This often will attract the wrong attention. You don't want your résumé to be passed around for the wrong reasons. A large defense contractor has what it calls the "Résumé of the Week." A recent one ended with the statement "Ask me how I lost 50 pounds."

11. Pay attention to the appearance of your résumé. Avoid overcrowding. Leave at least one-inch margins on the top, bottom, and sides. Underline, capitalize, and use bold print for emphasis. Always—and it should go without saying—type your résumé or have it printed. Believe it or not, a telecommunications organization recently received a résumé that was written in pencil.

12. Make sure your résumé is easy to read. Recruiters may read hundreds of résumés a week, and this can cause eyestrain. If your résumé is difficult to read—for example, if it doesn't have enough white space or the paragraphs are too thick—a recruiter may pass over it and never see your qualifications.

13. Bullets are eye-catching. Use a small "o" and fill in carefully with a black felt pen. Other alternatives are the asterisk (*) and the dash (-).

14. You have just gone through a great deal of effort to write your résumé. File your working papers and information in an accessible location and plan on updating them each year.

15. It goes without saying that you should never claim degrees, work experiences, and activities that you don't or didn't have. Unfortunately, this is a growing problem and a number of résumé verification firms have sprung up that are retained by employers to verify claims of college degrees, work accomplishments, or other facts.

Questions Please

Question: What if a company I have worked for in the past has merged with another company or been bought out and has changed names?

Answer: Use the new name of the company and beneath it add the old name.

Enterprises Unlimited
(formerly Gomez Business Consultants)

Question: Do I need a cover letter?

Answer: Never send a résumé without a cover letter. The cover letter needs to effectively draw attention to your résumé—one of hundreds that will be scanned.

Question: I graduated from college a long time ago. Can I eliminate the date that I received my degree? I am afraid that I will be discriminated against because of my age.

Answer: You can omit the date of your graduation, but, if you do, you run a greater risk that people will assume that you are hiding something. They may think that you are even older than you are!

Question: I am presently pursuing a degree. Should I include this information or will recruiters be put off wondering why it isn't finished?

Answer: If the degree will be in a relevant field, I would include it. Format it the same as you would a completed degree, but state, "Bachelor of Arts degree in progress." Or give the date when the degree is anticipated.

Question: I am a member of a minority group. Should I send a picture with my résumé so that I might get employment priority?

Answer: No. Although the law offers you equality, the truth is that many people are prejudiced. Why give people information that is not required and give them the opportunity to discriminate against you without even meeting you?

Question: I know it is illegal for an employer to ask about marriage and children, but some employers discriminate against women with children. Should I indicate on my résumé that I am married and childless?

Answer: No. If an employer doesn't want to hire women with children, he or she may still discriminate against you. Just because you don't have children now doesn't mean you don't plan on having them in the future.

Question: Should I include citizenship on my résumé?

Answer: Citizenship information is usually required on a job application. Although it is not required on a résumé, you might want to include this information if:

1. You have studied or lived outside the United States for much of your life and you would like to clarify citizenship.
2. You are interested is working for a company that is a major defense contractor.

Question: I completed a one-year program at a noncollege professional school. I am no longer in that career field and it has no bearing on my present career objective. Do I need to include this?

Answer: No. If you feel that this program doesn't support your career goals, you don't have to include it. Be prepared to explain the one-year gap and why you have omitted this from your résumé. I omitted a professional school from my résumé, and in ten years, no one has ever questioned the one-year gap.

Question: Do I list salary on my résumé or send a salary history?

Answer: No. Salary is something to discuss during the interview. Some companies run classified ads requesting salary history when they have no intention of hiring. They're interested in current salaries to revamp their compensation plans. Even if you know there is a legitimate job opportunity, I still advise individuals not to discuss salary until the interview.

Question: I have been out of work for nine months. How do I show or explain this work gap?

Answer: Some employers give severance and vacation pay upon termination. This time period can be added to your dates of employment and it will narrow the gap. What have you been doing during this transition period? Any professional development? Dan Adams began work on a book while he was looking for work and Jack Klein began a master's degree in his field. Both of these experiences were included on their résumés. It filled the work gap and provided interesting information to discuss during an interview. Use the following experiences to fill a work gap: consultant, self-employed, writer, student, researcher, or traveler.

Question: I have heard of a vita or curriculum vitae. Do I use this or a résumé?

Answer: A vita or curriculum vitae is defined as an autobiographical sketch that is used for professionals such as doctors, dentists, or college professors. It includes education, publications, licenses, and board certifications.

Question: How far back do I go?

Answer: There is no definite answer. Ask yourself, "How relevant is the experience to the position I am seeking?" Include it if it is still valid and meaningful. Don't include it if it isn't. Experience can still be valid, but if you have more current experience, you may want to delete the older, repetitious experience.

Question: How can I indicate that I have received numerous promotions?

Answer: Make a statement within the experience section, for example:

Promoted three times to increasingly responsible positions.
Promoted to this position.

See the résumé on page 78.

Question: Should I include military service on my résumé?

Answer: Include military service if it is relevant to the type of organization or field you are interested in, such as law enforcement, defense contractor, security and safety, or public service. Military service is always included on an application.

Question: Is it acceptable to use jargon for computer and technical fields?

Answer: Use acronyms and jargon for universally accepted software, hardware, and systems (for example, BASIC or IBM PC). Beware of using jargon when changing fields, industries, or moving from the public to private sector (or vice versa).

Question: How should I show computer literacy or expertise, other than a separate skills section?

Answer: Incorporate the information into your experience, education, or training sections, for example, "Prepare reports using LOTUS 123."

2 Before and After— Résumé Makeovers

A picture is worth a thousand words. I can give you all the principles in the world on writing effective résumés, but if you never see them properly applied, it is difficult to envision the end result.

Marketing experts have long known the value of "before and after" pictures in revealing possibilities. Most of us can benefit from assistance and that is particularly true of résumés. Let's look at some sample résumés and see how they could be improved to demonstrate principles important in your own résumé development.

Many of these résumés are based on actual samples brought to training classes. The real names and basic facts about the individuals have been changed to protect their privacy.

For each example, an original résumé is introduced. Next, comments on the résumé are given to highlight weaknesses and to point out areas where it might be improved. Finally, a revised résumé is presented, implementing the suggestions.

RÉSUMÉ INDEX

OCCUPATIONS	Page No.	Chronological	Functional	Career Objective	Career Summary
Administrative Assistant	138	X		X	
Adult Education Director	115	X			X
Association Executive	110	X			
Auditor	103	X		X	
Controller	73	X		X	
Economist	67	X		X	
Financial Manager	32	X		X	
Health Care Administrator	37		X		
Insurance Manager	120	X			X
Lawyer	97	X			X
Marketing Manager	70	X			
Marketing Specialist	57	X			X
Management Consultant	78	X			X
Personnel Manager	146		X		
Police Officer	62		X	X	
Product Planner	70		X	X	
Public Relations Manager	47	X			
Purchasing Director	126	X			
Retail Manager	92	X		X	

OCCUPATIONS	Page No.	Chronological	Functional	Career Objective	Career Summary
Sales Manager	83	X			X
Special Education Administrator	141	X			X
Systems Development Supervisor	89	X			X
Systems Support Manager	53	X			X
Teacher	42	X		X	X
Temporary Placement Manager	135	X			X
Trainer	131		X	X	

PETER M. MARTIN

---

45 Peachtree Lane, Atlanta, Georgia 30045
(404) 566-6661 (h) (404) 563-3789 (w)

CAREER OBJECTIVE: A financial management position.

EXPERIENCE

Atlanta Savings and Loan, Atlanta, Georgia

Accounting Manager
Report to the Chief Financial Officer. Management responsibility
for all accounting functions and a staff of 10. Ensure that all
reports are completed in an accurate and timely manner
and accounting procedures and internal controls are in place. Work
with external auditors and examiners. 1985-present

Auditor
Reported to the Director of Internal Audit. Responsible for
supervising all audit activities (including financial and
operational reviews) for field and home office audit programs.
1983-1985

Arthur Andersen & Co., Atlanta, Georgia

Accountant
Took client information to prepare individual tax returns and
coordinated the preparation and review of returns for Trust
Department clients. 1981-1983

EDUCATION/CERTIFICATION

Masters in Business Administration, University of Georgia,
Atlanta, Georgia, 1981

Bachelor of Science in Accounting, University of Georgia,
Atlanta, Georgia, 1979

Associate in Applied Science, Taylor Community College, Atlanta,
Georgia, 1977

Certified Public Accountant (CPA)

Certified Management Accountant (CMA)

PROFESSIONAL ASSOCIATIONS

American Institute of Certified Public Accountants
Georgia Society of Management Accountants
University of Georgia Alumni Association

PETER M. MARTIN

45 Peachtree Lane, Atlanta, Georgia 30045
(404) 566-6661 (h) (404) 563-3789 (w)

1. If you are going to use a career objective, try to make it more specific.

(1) CAREER OBJECTIVE: A financial management position.

EXPERIENCE

Atlanta Savings and Loan, Atlanta, Georgia

2. What type of bank is this? Large? Small? What type of revenues? Don't begin with "Report to"—that takes away from your responsibilities.

(2) Accounting Manager
Report to the Chief Financial Officer. Management responsibility for all accounting functions and a staff of 10. Ensure that all reports are completed in an accurate and timely manner (3) and accounting procedures and internal controls are in place. Work with external auditors and examiners. 1985-present

3. This sounds like a clerk, not a manager.

Auditor
Reported to the Director of Internal Audit. Responsible for (4) supervising all audit activities (including financial and operational reviews) for field and home office audit programs. 1983-1985

4. Experience areas need to be expanded. There needs to be more meat. What does the supervision of all audit activities include?

Arthur Andersen & Co., Atlanta, Georgia

Accountant
Took client information to prepare individual tax returns and coordinated the preparation and review of returns for Trust (4) Department clients. 1981-1983

5. Combine these two as the degrees were received at the same university.

EDUCATION/CERTIFICATION

Masters in Business Administration, University of Georgia, Atlanta, Georgia, 1981
(5)
Bachelor of Science in Accounting, University of Georgia, Atlanta, Georgia, 1979

6. Delete the associate's degree. Since there is a master's degree, it doesn't add to the credentials.

(6) Associate in Applied Science, Taylor Community College, Atlanta, Georgia, 1977

7. Include separately under "Licenses." These credentials can also be added after the name.

Certified Public Accountant (CPA)
(7)
Certified Management Accountant (CMA)

8. Delete the alumni association.

PROFESSIONAL ASSOCIATIONS

American Institute of Certified Public Accountants
Georgia Society of Management Accountants
(8) University of Georgia Alumni Association

Comments: The résumé is unappealing in format and content. This individual's credentials and expertise need to be emphasized.

PETER M. MARTIN CPA CMA
45 Peachtree Lane
Atlanta, Georgia 30045
(404) 566-6661 (h) (404) 563-3789 (w)

CAREER OBJECTIVE

A position as a financial manager with a multi-national corporation in the service industry.

EXPERIENCE

Atlanta Savings and Loan, Atlanta, Georgia

Accounting Manager 1985 - present

Direct responsibility for all accounting functions for a bank with revenues of $50 million. Oversee the completion of regulatory and internal reports, implement new accounting procedures and internal controls, and assist the external auditors and examiners. Manage staff of ten.

Chaired a task force that streamlined reporting process; saved organization $250,000.

Auditor 1983 - 1985

Developed and implemented a comprehensive audit program; reviewed the internal control system, revised the audit report format, and made presentations to the Audit Committee of the Board of Directors. Identified and resolved problems with the accounting system through recommendations to the Information Systems Manager.

Arthur Andersen & Co., Atlanta, Georgia

Accountant 1981-1983

Prepared and reviewed tax returns for individual clients and managed the preparation and review of returns for all of the Trust Department customers of Atlanta Savings and Loan. Interviewed clients to gather tax information, researched tax questions, and advised clients on tax laws. Assisted clients with Internal Revenue Service audits and coordinated and reviewed returns that were prepared through a computerized tax service.

EDUCATION

University of Georgia, Atlanta, Georgia

Masters in Business Administration, 1981. Graduated Magna Cum Laude

Bachelor of Science in Accounting, 1979

Professional Training: Numerous seminars in taxes, auditing, computers and management skills

PROFESSIONAL CERTIFICATIONS

Certified Public Accountant
Certified Management Accountant

PROFESSIONAL ASSOCIATIONS

American Institute of Certified Public Accountants
Georgia Society of Management Accountants

Janice Brinker, M.S.

7784 Wandering Way,   Topeka, Kansas 66614   (913) 988-1452

CAREER OBJECTIVE

Seeking career advancement in the increasingly competitive and expanding field of healthcare management.

EDUCATION

M.S.: Health; Nebraska State, Wichita, Nebraska. 1980.
B.S.: Health, Physical Education and Recreation; Nebraska State, Wichita, Nebraska. 1978.
Internship: The American Hospital, Paris, France. 1978.

EXPERIENCE

Project Director/Ambulatory Services: Twin Oaks Medical Center, 25 Main Street, Topeka, KS. 2/87-present

President: Health Promotion Consultants, P.O. Box 63, Topeka, KS. 6/86- 2/87

Director: The Plains Recreation Center, P.O. Box 900, Emporia, KS. 2/85- 6/86

Health Educator: County Health Department, 77 First Street, Emporia, KS. 9/83-2/85

Safety Instructor: American Red Cross, Emporia, KS. 1/83-9/83

Marketing/Sales Representative: John Hancock, Dodge City, KS. 12/81- 12/82

Eligibility Counselor: Kansas Social Services, Topeka, KS. 6/81-12/81

Substitute Teacher: Topeka City Schools, Topeka, KS. 9/80-5/81

PROFESSIONAL DEVELOPMENT

American Hospital Association: Society for Ambulatory Care Professionals Continuing Ed. Conf., 1988.
Kans. Hospital Association: Attracting Women's Healthcare Market, 1987; Product Line Mgmt., 1987.
Dale Carnegie: Effective Speaking and Human Relations, 1986.

OTHER

Professional Organizations: American Heart Assoc., American Red Cross; League of Women Voters; Society for Ambulatory Care Prof., Kans. Hospital Assoc., Young Hospital Administrators.
Community Committee Activities: American Red Cross Safety Committee, 1986-88; Metropolitan Council Red Cross Study Committee, 1987; United Way Allocations Committee, 1987-88.

AMPLIFIED RECORD OF EXPERIENCE

<u>Project Director/Ambulatory Services</u>: Twin Oaks Medical Center. 2/87- 6/88.

As a member of the management team responsible for directing the overall marketing and planning for the Ambulatory Services. General responsibilities included planning of all marketing campaigns, proposing new areas of revenue growth, strategic planning, and medical staff planning and budget development. During this time the following projects were accomplished:

* Acted as liaison to physicians and their staff. Made 'sales calls' to physicians and staff regarding level of satisfaction of our services. Planned and implemented luncheon seminars for office staff of physicians. Topics were related to hospital services. Seminars were well attended and resulted in stronger relationships with physicians office staff.

* Developed and implemented a mammography campaign which resulted in an increase of mammography studies of 238% the first month offered, leveling off at monthly increases of 150% thereafter, establishing our center in the consumers' eyes.

* Developed numerous marketing materials including pens, pads, etc. for the physicians and their staff. Also developed brochures for Mammography, MRI as well as others.

<u>President</u>: Health Promotion Consultants. 6/86-2/87.

Responsible for securing consulting contracts and implementing projects. During this time the following contracts were completed:

* ABH, Inc., Topeka, KS. Research project which required designing a data base to allow client to access information and make decisions on whether 'treatment' was needed.

* JGG Marketing Network. Developed data base for marketing research. Information was developed for a 13-county area.

<u>Director</u>: The Plains Recreation Center. 2/85-6/86.

Responsible for entire operation of $2 million employee recreation/fitness facility. General responsibilities included supervision of 3 full time and 30 part time employees, creating, planning, implementing fitness/recreational programs, marketing services to eligible participants, and budget development. During this time period the following projects were accomplished:

*Coordinated the final construction of the facility which included securing bids for jobs, designing and overseeing work.

*Researched and coordinated the purchase of $80K in additional equipment which ultimately lead to 60% in utilization of the facility.

<u>Health Educator</u>: County Health Department. 9/83-2/85

Responsible for various health promotion programs and completed the following projects:

* Received funding for a county wide safety belt program which consisted of friendly reminder signs 'We need you, buckle up'. This resulted in a state wide program.

* Coordinated safety belt competition for 11 area high schools. Over $20K was raised.

<u>Safety Instructor</u>. American Red Cross. 1/83-9/83.

Instructed Cardiopulmonary Resuscitation (CPR), First Aid and Water Safety classes; developed lesson plans/goals for classes.

<u>Marketing/Sales Representative</u>. John Hancock. 12/81-12/82.

Developed advertising materials; implemented advertising campaigns; represented agency in community and civic activities; sold property and casualty insurance on commission basis; supervised three employees.

<u>Eligibility Counselor</u>: Kansas Social Services. 6/81-5/81.

Interviewed welfare and food stamp applicants; determined eligibility.

<u>Substitute Teacher</u>: Topeka City Schools. 9/80-5/81.

Taught class in absence of regular instructor; followed instructors lesson plans; assisted students with assignments.

1. This is too large and overwhelming.

2. Place education after experience. It is already indicated in the heading that the individual has an M.S. degree.

3. Eliminate addresses.

4. The credentials and experience are strong enough without this. Eliminate.

5. This would be included in lieu of credentials, but it is not needed. Include this information on an application instead.

① Janice Brinker, M.S.

7784 Wandering Way,   Topeka, Kansas 66614   (913) 988-1452

CAREER OBJECTIVE

Seeking career advancement in the increasingly competitive and expanding field of healthcare management.

② EDUCATION

M.S.: Health; Nebraska State, Wichita, Nebraska. 1980.
B.S.: Health, Physical Education and Recreation; Nebraska State, Wichita, Nebraska. 1978.
Internship: The American Hospital, Paris, France. 1978.

EXPERIENCE ③

Project Director/Ambulatory Services: Twin Oaks Medical Center, 25 Main Street, Topeka, KS. 2/87-present

President: Health Promotion Consultants, P.O. Box 63, Topeka, KS. 6/86- 2/87

Director: The Plains Recreation Center, P.O. Box 900, Emporia, KS. 2/85- 6/86

Health Educator: County Health Department, 77 First Street, Emporia, KS. 9/83-2/85

Safety Instructor: American Red Cross, Emporia, KS. 1/83-9/83

Marketing/Sales Representative: John Hancock, Dodge City, KS. 12/81- 12/82

Eligibility Counselor: Kansas Social Services, Topeka, KS. 6/81-12/81

Substitute Teacher: Topeka City Schools, Topeka, KS. 9/80-5/81

④ PROFESSIONAL DEVELOPMENT

American Hospital Association: Society for Ambulatory Care Professionals Continuing Ed. Conf., 1988.
Kans. Hospital Association: Attracting Women's Healthcare Market, 1987; Product Line Mgmt., 1987.
Dale Carnegie: Effective Speaking and Human Relations, 1986.

⑤ OTHER

Professional Organizations: American Heart Assoc., American Red Cross; League of Women Voters; Society for Ambulatory Care Prof., Kans. Hospital Assoc., Young Hospital Administrators.
Community Committee Activities: American Red Cross Safety Committee, 1986-88; Metropolitan Council Red Cross Study Committee, 1987; United Way Allocations Committee, 1987-88.

6. This information should be included under "Experience."

7. "Developed and implemented" is redundant.

8. This position can be deleted. Discuss it during the interview.

9. These positions can be deleted.

(6) AMPLIFIED RECORD OF EXPERIENCE

Project Director/Ambulatory Services: Twin Oaks Medical Center. 2/87- 6/88.

As a member of the management team responsible for directing the overall marketing and planning for the Ambulatory Services. General responsibilities included planning of all marketing campaigns, proposing new areas of revenue growth, strategic planning, and medical staff planning and budget development. During this time the following projects were accomplished:

* Acted as liaison to physicians and their staff. Made 'sales calls' to physicians and staff regarding level of satisfaction of our services. Planned and implemented luncheon seminars for office staff of physicians. Topics were related to hospital services. Seminars were well attended and resulted in stronger relationships with physicians office staff.

(7) * Developed and implemented a mammography campaign which resulted in an increase of mammography studies of 238% the first month offered, leveling off at monthly increases of 150% thereafter, establishing our center in the consumers' eyes.

* Developed numerous marketing materials including pens, pads, etc. for the physicians and their staff. Also developed brochures for Mammography, MRI as well as others.

President: Health Promotion Consultants. 6/86-2/87.

Responsible for securing consulting contracts and implementing projects. During this time the following contracts were completed:

* ABH, Inc., Topeka, KS. Research project which required designing a data base to allow client to access information and make decisions on whether 'treatment' was needed.
* JGG Marketing Network. Developed data base for marketing research. Information was developed for a 13-county area.

Director: The Plains Recreation Center. 2/85-6/86.

Responsible for entire operation of $2 million employee recreation/fitness facility. General responsibilities included supervision of 3 full time and 30 part time employees, creating, planning, implementing fitness/recreational programs, marketing services to eligible participants, and budget development. During this time period the following projects were accomplished:

*Coordinated the final construction of the facility which included securing bids for jobs, designing and overseeing work.

*Researched and coordinated the purchase of $80K in additional equipment which ultimately lead to 60% in utilization of the facility.

Health Educator: County Health Department. 9/83-2/85

Responsible for various health promotion programs and completed the following projects:

* Received funding for a county wide safety belt program which consisted of friendly reminder signs 'We need you, buckle up'. This resulted in a state wide program.
* Coordinated safety belt competition for 11 area high schools. Over $20K was raised.

(8) Safety Instructor. American Red Cross. 1/83-9/83.

Instructed Cardiopulmonary Resuscitation (CPR), First Aid and Water Safety classes; developed lesson plans/goals for classes.

Marketing/Sales Representative. John Hancock. 12/81-12/82.

Developed advertising materials; implemented advertising campaigns; represented agency in community and civic activities; sold property and casualty insurance on commission basis; supervised three employees.

Eligibility Counselor: Kansas Social Services. 6/81-5/81.

(9) Interviewed welfare and food stamp applicants; determined eligibility.

Substitute Teacher: Topeka City Schools. 9/80-5/81.

Taught class in absence of regular instructor; followed instructors lesson plans; assisted students with assignments.

Comments: The type is too small and difficult to read. The résumé is out of balance. Experience sections need to be shortened and those not relevant to career goals omitted.

Janice Brinker, M.S.

7784 Wandering Way Topeka, Kansas 66614 (913) 988-1452

Health Care Administrator

PROFESSIONAL EXPERIENCE

Management

Managed overall marketing and planning for amubulatory departments: supervised employees, planned marketing campaigns, proposed new areas of revenue growth, strategic and medical staff planning, and budget development.

Prepared new job descriptions for business and clinical staff.

Operated $2 million employee recreation/fitness facility; supervised three full-time and 30 part-time employees; created, planned, and implemented fitness/recreational programs; marketed services to eligible participants and developed budgets.

Program Development

Established data base for marketing research for 13-county area in Kansas and Missouri.

Developed proposals for future growth and development of Ambulatory operations; re-designed physical areas and incorporated new computer system.

Raised over $20K for safety belt competition program for 11 area high schools.

Researched and coordinated the purchase of additional equipment; experienced 60% increase in utilization of facility.

Marketing

Initiated and implemented a mammography campaign which resulted in an increase of mammography studies of 238% the first month offered, leveling off at monthly increases of 150%. Created brochures for Mammography, MRI, and Dental Implants.

Designed format for tracking physicians usage in Ambulatory Services using dBase software.

EMPLOYMENT HISTORY

Project Director/Ambulatory Services: Twin Oaks Medical Center, Topeka, Kansas 1987-present
President: Health Promotion Consultants, Topeka, Kansas 1986-1987
Director: The Plains Recreation Center, Emporia, Kansas 1985-1986
Health Educator: County Health Department, Emporia, Kansas 1983-1985
Marketing/Sales Representative: John Hancock, Dodge City, Kansas 1981- 1982
Internship: The American Hospital, Paris, France 1978.

EDUCATION

Nebraska State, Wichita, Nebraska.
Master of Science, Health, 1980.
Bachelor of Science, Health, Physical Education,Recreation, 1978.

——— Maria H. Diaz ——
   98 Locust Avenue, Los Angeles, California (213) 778-4556

Professional Experience

1979 - present	Part-time Instructor in Mathematics, Los Angeles Junior College, Los Angeles, CA. Subjects taught: Elementary Algebra, Intermediate Algebra, Trigonometry, Finite Math, Math for General Education. I have also researched and chosen textbooks for Finite Math and Math for General Education.
1976 - 1979	Adjunct Instructor in Mathematics, Los Almos Community College, Los Almos, CA. Subjects taught: Elementary Algebra, Trigonometry, Pre-Calculus. I also worked with students taking self-paced course options.
1974 - 1976	Home Tutor, Thompkins Board of Education, Thompkins, CA. Taught all subjects to students in grades 7-12 who were unable to attend school. I worked with teachers, parents, as well as students, in coordinating their school work.
1974 - 1976	Substitute Teacher, Thompkins Board of Education, Thompkins, CA.
1969 - 1970	Mathematics Teacher, Los Angeles Board of Education, Los Angeles, CA. Taught students in grades 7 and 8 of all abilities.
1968 - 1969	Mathematics Teacher, Orange County Board of Education, San Francisco, CA. Taught students in grades 9 and 10 of all abilities.

Educational Background

1967 - 1968	Master of Education in Mathematics, including 15 credits in advanced mathematics. University of California, Berkeley, California.
1963 - 1967	B. A. Major: Education Minor: Mathematics (33 credits) State University College, Geneseo, New York

Additional Educational Experiences

1984 - 1985   Auditting Calculus 65A and 65B, Los Angeles Junior
               College, Los Angeles, California.

1984   BASIC Programming Course, Continuing Education,
               Los Angeles, California.

1979   Fortran Computer Science Course, Los Almos State
               College, Los Almos, California.

1976 - 1978   Nineteen credits in Accounting Classes, Los Almos
               Community College, Los Almos, California.

Certification

California Community College Credential in Mathematics
New York Teaching Credential for Mathematics, Grades 7 to 12

Professional Associations

California Mathematics Council for Community Colleges
Mathematics Association of America

Community Activities

Volunteer Mathematics Enrichment Teacher, C. L. Terry Elementary
   School, 1980-1985
C. L. Terry PTA President, 1983-1985.
C. L. Terry PTA Historian, 1982-1983.
Morris Junior High PTA Historian, 1982-1983.
Girl Scout Leader, 1977-1985.
Age Level Consultant for the Los Angeles Girl Scout Service
   Unit Team, 1982-1985.
Treasurer, Los Almos State College Figure Skating Club, 1977-1979.
Chairperson of Religious School Committee, Los Almos, CA, 1976-1979.

Placement Credentials are on file at: Career Planning and Placement
                                      State University College
                                      Geneseo, NY 12405

Comments

1. Eliminate the word "part-time"— experience is experience whether it is full-time, part-time, paid, or unpaid.

2. Either the position or the organization should be highlighted.

3. "Taught" is redundant.

4. Eliminate pronouns.

5. This should have some explanation.

6. Degree and school should be separate and on different lines.

7. Spell out "Bachelor of Arts."

8. Inconsistent. Format all education the same.

9. Group positions.

10. Margins are wide and out of balance.

——— Maria H. Diaz ———————————————————
98 Locust Avenue, Los Angeles, California (213) 778-4556

<u>Professional Experience</u> ①

1979 - present   Part-time Instructor in Mathematics, Los Angeles Junior College, Los Angeles, CA. Subjects taught: Elementary Algebra, Intermediate Algebra, Trigonometry, Finite Math, Math for General Education. I have also researched and chosen textbooks for Finite Math and Math for General Education.

1976 - 1979   ② ③ Adjunct Instructor in Mathematics, Los Almos Community College, Los Almos, CA. Subjects taught: Elementary Algebra, Trigonometry, Pre-Calculus. I also worked with students taking self-paced/course options.

1974 - 1976   ② ④ Home Tutor, Thompkins Board of Education, Thompkins, CA. Taught all subjects to students in grades 7-12 who were unable to attend school. I worked with teachers, parents, as well as students, in coordinating their school work.

1974 - 1976   ⑤ Substitute Teacher, Thompkins Board of Education, Thompkins, CA.

1969 - 1970   ⑨ Mathematics Teacher, Los Angeles Board of Education, Los Angeles, CA. Taught students in grades 7 and 8 of all abilities.

1968 - 1969   Mathematics Teacher, Orange County Board of Education, San Francisco, CA. Taught students in grades 9 and 10 of all abilities.

<u>Educational Background</u>

1967 - 1968   ⑥ Master of Education in Mathematics, including 15 credits in advanced mathematics. University of California, Berkeley, California.

1963 - 1967   ⑦ ⑧ B. A. Major: Education
         Minor: Mathematics (33 credits)
State University College, Geneseo, New York

⑩

11. Spelling error.

12. These experiences are important but they take up more room than the bachelor's and master's degrees. Are they more important? Format accordingly.

13. Does this make the individual a more qualified candidate? A more appropriate place for this information may be the application.

Additional Educational Experiences

1984 - 1985	⑪	Auditting Calculus 65A and 65B, Los Angeles Junior College, Los Angeles, California.
1984		BASIC Programming Course, Continuing Education, Los Angeles, California.
1979		Fortran Computer Science Course, Los Almos State College, Los Almos, California.
1976 - 1978		Nineteen credits in Accounting Classes, Los Almos Community College, Los Almos, California.

⑫

Certification

California Community College Credential in Mathematics
New York Teaching Credential for Mathematics, Grades 7 to 12

Professional Associations

California Mathematics Council for Community Colleges
Mathematics Association of America

Community Activities

Volunteer Mathematics Enrichment Teacher, C. L. Terry Elementary
    School, 1980-1985.
C. L. Terry PTA President, 1983-1985.
C. L. Terry PTA Historian, 1982-1983.
⑬ Morris Junior High PTA Historian, 1982-1983.
Girl Scout Leader, 1977-1985.
Age Level Consultant for the Los Angeles Girl Scout Service
    Unit Team, 1982-1985.
Treasurer, Los Almos State College Figure Skating Club, 1977-1979.
Chairperson of Religious School Committee, Los Almos, CA, 1976-1979.

Placement Credentials are on file at: Career Planning and Placement
                                        State University College
                                        Geneseo, NY 12405

Comments: This résumé can be effective and easy to read on one page.

MARIA H. DIAZ

98 Locust Avenue   (213)778-4556 (h)
Los Angeles, California 90030   (213)921-7322 (w)

CAREER OBJECTIVE

A position as a mathematics instructor in higher education.

SYNOPSIS OF EXPERIENCE

20 years experience in mathematics education. Subjects taught include:

Elementary Algebra	Trigonometry	Intermediate Algebra
Pre-Calculus	Finite Math	Math for General Education

PROFESSIONAL EXPERIENCE

Mathematics Instructor, 1979–present
Los Angeles Junior College, Los Angeles, California

Adjunct Mathematics Instructor, 1976–1979
Los Almos Junior College, Los Almos, California

Home Tutor, 1974–1976
Substitute Teacher, 1975–1976
Thompkins Board of Education, Thompkins, California

Mathematices Teacher, 1969–1970
Los Angeles Board of Education, Los Angeles, California

Mathematics Teacher, 1968–1969
Orange County Board of Education, San Francisco, California

EDUCATION

Master of Education in Mathematics, 1968
University of California, Berkeley, California
Includes 15 credits in advanced mathematics

Bachelor of Arts in Education, minor in Mathematics, 1967
State University College, Geneseo, New York
Includes 33 credits in mathematics

Continuing Education:
Audited Calculus 65A and 65B at Los Angeles Junior College;
19 credits in Accounting; BASIC and Fortran

CERTIFICATION

California Community College Credential in Mathematics

New York Teaching Credential for Mathematics, Grades 7 to 12

PROFESSIONAL ASSOCIATIONS

California Mathematics Council for Community Colleges

Mathematics Association of America

Placement Credentials on file at: Career Planning and Placement,
State University College, Geneseo, New York 12045

LOUISE PLANTAIN
66 Rocky Bluff
Bangor, Maine 04401
(207) 229-9988

Career Objective
Seeking to advance my career in the increasingly competitive and
expanding marketing, public relations and communications field.

Experience

Director of Marketing
1986-1989

Bangor Medical Center   296 beds
Bangor, Maine   90 beds

   As a member of the administrative staff responsible for directing
the overall marketing activities for two of HCA's healthcare
facilities. General responsibilities include planning of all
communications and marketing campaigns, proposing new areas of
revenue growth, strategic planning, medical staff planning and
development, overseeing all public relations and employee
functions, and media relations.
     During this time accomplished the following additional
projects:
  • Developed and implemented a Day Surgery Campaign which
    resulted in an increase of over 1,000 new cases and
    approximately $1.8 million in gross revenues over a 12 month
    period.
  • Designed, wrote, and implemented a computer program that
    tracked physician admissions and revenues by individual
    physician, physician practice group, and medical specialty.
  • Standardized many of the monthly and annual physician,
    employee, and community events so that they would be cost and
    time efficient.
  • Designed and implemented an agency project format within the
    department so that each project could be reviewed and tracked.
  • Developed a physician relations "sales team" to inform the
    medical staff and their respective office staffs of the
    specific services available, how to utilize these services and
    to collect information on how we could better serve their
    needs.

Memberships and Associations:
Vice President of Finance and Membership of the International
Association of Business Communicators; Member of American Marketing
Association, Maine Hospital Association, American Hospital
Association, and American Hospital Association Society for
Healthcare Planning and Marketing.

43

Director of Marketing/Public Relations
1984-1986

Portland Medical Center   597 beds
Portland, Maine

Responsible for assessing, creating, and implementing a full
marketing/communications program including: community, industrial,
employee, physician, patient, and media relations.
        In addition accomplished the following projects:
    • Implemented a monthly public education program that drew over
      500 people per month and generated approximately 8-12
      admissions per month from this program.
    • Maintained market share of admissions and revenue after a new
      hospital was opened in our marketplace.
    • Worked with the news media to minimize the effects of a highly
      publicized case involving a 4-year old burn victim that was
      denied admission.
    • Developed marketing campaign for a new medical building that
      resulted in 85 percent occupancy when opened.

Director of Public Relations/Marketing
1982-1984

St. Mary's Medical Center   396 beds
Concord, New Hampshire

Directed the overall communications and public relations functions
of the hospital. Responsible for developing and implementing an
ongoing program for the hospital's internal and external publics.

Public Relations Supervisor
1977-1982

Manchester Hospital   596 beds
Manchester, New Hampshire

    • Managed the production of all audiovisual, video, and multi-
      media productions and their respective scripts.
    • Responsible for developing a continuous working relationship
      with the news medias to explain the complicated world of
      medicine and the various misconceptions regarding the medical
      and hospital communities.

EDUCATION

1976-1977:   New Hampshire College, Manchester, New Hampshire
                    Master of Arts Degree in Communications

1972-1976:   Concord State, Concord, New Hampshire
                    Bachelor of Arts Degree in Psychology

1. This wording is very self-serving.

2. Include the bed size in the text—it looks funny over by itself.

3. This is too wordy. Simplify with active verb.

4. Delete this sentence and double-space to highlight the accomplishments.

5. This doesn't belong in the middle of the experience section. Place it later in the résumé.

LOUISE PLANTAIN
66 Rocky Bluff
Bangor, Maine 04401
(207) 229-9988

Career Objective (1)
Seeking to advance my career in the increasingly competitive and expanding marketing, public relations and communications field.

Experience

Director of Marketing
1986–1989

Bangor Medical Center   296 beds (2)
Bangor, Maine   90 beds

As a member of the administrative staff responsible for directing (3) the overall marketing activities for two of HCA's healthcare facilities. General responsibilities include planning of all communications and marketing campaigns, proposing new areas of revenue growth, strategic planning, medical staff planning and development, overseeing all public relations and employee functions, and media relations.

During this time accomplished the following additional projects:
(4) • Developed and implemented a Day Surgery Campaign which resulted in an increase of over 1,000 new cases and approximately $1.8 million in gross revenues over a 12 month period.
   • Designed, wrote, and implemented a computer program that tracked physician admissions and revenues by individual physician, physician practice group, and medical specialty.
   • Standardized many of the monthly and annual physician, employee, and community events so that they would be cost and time efficient.
   • Designed and implemented an agency project format within the department so that each project could be reviewed and tracked.
   • Developed a physician relations "sales team" to inform the medical staff and their respective office staffs of the specific services available, how to utilize these services and to collect information on how we could better serve their needs.

(5) Memberships and Associations:
Vice President of Finance and Membership of the International Association of Business Communicators; Member of American Marketing Association, Maine Hospital Association, American Hospital Association, and American Hospital Association Society for Healthcare Planning and Marketing.

6. Express more concisely. Double-space before the accomplishments.

7. This sounds like a job description.

8. This doesn't read well at all—express this better or omit.

9. Use dates of graduation only.

Director of Marketing/Public Relations
1984–1986

Portland Medical Center   (2) 597 beds
Portland, Maine
(6)
Responsible for assessing, creating, and implementing a full
marketing/communications program including: community, industrial,
employee, physician, patient, and media relations.
    In addition accomplished the following projects:
  • Implemented a monthly public education program that drew over
    500 people per month and generated approximately 8–12
    admissions per month from this program.
  • Maintained market share of admissions and revenue after a new
    hospital was opened in our marketplace.
  • Worked with the news media to minimize the effects of a highly
    publicized case involving a 4-year old burn victim that was
    denied admission.
  • Developed marketing campaign for a new medical building that
    resulted in 85 percent occupancy when opened.

Director of Public Relations/Marketing
1982–1984

St. Mary's Medical Center   396 beds (2)
Concord, New Hampshire

Directed the overall communications and public relations functions)
of the hospital. Responsible for developing and implementing an   } (7)
ongoing program for the hospital's internal and external publics.   )

Public Relations Supervisor
1977–1982

Manchester Hospital   596 beds (2)
Manchester, New Hampshire

  • Managed the production of all audiovisual, video, and multi-
    media productions and their respective scripts.
  • Responsible for developing a continuous working relationship   )
    with the news medias to explain the complicated world of   } (8)
    medicine and the various misconceptions regarding the medical   )
    and hospital communities.

EDUCATION

1976–1977:   New Hampshire College, Manchester, New Hampshire
(9)   Master of Arts Degree in Communications

1972–1976:   Concord State, Concord, New Hampshire
                  Bachelor of Arts Degree in Psychology

Comments: The résumé is difficult to read and cluttered. Better
format, layout, and organization are needed.

LOUISE PLANTAIN

66 Rocky Bluff, Bangor, Maine 04401 (207) 229-9988

EXPERIENCED MARKETING/PUBLIC RELATIONS PROFESSIONAL

EXPERIENCE

DIRECTOR OF MARKETING, 1986-1990

Bangor Medical Center, Bangor, Maine

Directed the overall marketing activities for two healthcare facilities (296 bed and 90 bed). Planned all communications and marketing campaigns, proposed new areas for revenue growth, strategic and medical staff planning and development, and oversaw all public relations, employee functions, and media relations.

Developed and implemented a Day Surgery Campaign; increased new cases by over 1,000 and generated approximately $1.8 million in gross revenues over a 12 month period.

Designed, wrote, and implemented a computer program that tracked physician admissions and revenues by individual physician, physician practice group, and medical specialty.

Created a physician relations "Sales Team" to inform the medical staff and their respective office staffs of the specific services available, how to utilize the services, and to determine how we could better serve their needs.

Saved costs and time by standardizing many monthly and annual physician, employee, and community events.

DIRECTOR OF MARKETING/PUBLIC RELATIONS, 1984-1986

Portland Medical Center, Portland, Maine

Assessed, created, and implemented a full marketing/communications program that included community, industrial, employee, physician, patient, and media relations for a 597 bed hospital.

Initiated a monthly public education program that drew over 500 people per month; generated approximately 8-12 new admissions per month.

Maintained hospital's market share of admissions and revenue after new hospital opened in our marketplace.

DIRECTOR OF PUBLIC RELATIONS/MARKETING, 1982-1984

St. Mary's Medical Center, Concord, New Hampshire

Directed the overall communications and public relations functions of a 396 bed hospital.

PUBLIC RELATIONS SUPERVISOR, 1977-1982

Manchester Hospital, Manchester, New Hampshire

Managed the production of all audiovisual, video, and multi-media productions and their respective scripts for a 596 bed hospital. Established effective working relationships with the news media.

EDUCATION

Master of Arts in Communications, 1977
New Hampshire College, Manchester, New Hampshire

Bachelor of Arts in Psychology, 1976
Concord State, Concord, New Hampshire

ASSOCIATIONS

Vice-President of Finance and Membership, International Association of Business Communicators
American Marketing Association
Maine Hospital Association
American Hospital Association
Society for Healthcare Planning and Marketing

STANLEY HUNT
16731 Harris Street
Dallas, Texas 75222

Home: (214) 556-6789
Work: (214) 789-0077

OVERVIEW:

- Possess in-depth experience in management and finance for Sky Chef Corporation.
- Adaptable to new and changing environments; traveled extensively throughout the United States, Europe and South America to analyze inflight food services.
- Successful in utilizing strong public relations skills in communicating with foreign business persons, colleagues and general public.
- Proficient writer in preparing documentation of foreign and domestic evaluations with a fluency in French.

CAREER HIGHLIGHTS:

Sky Chef Corporation
Dallas, Texas
August 1973-present

Director of Systems Support, 1988-present
Direct all billing and computer applications for Inflight Catering Division (DEC: pricing, billing, inventory and requisitioning) with emphasis on coordinating all computer systems (main office computer tie-in to 60 satellite, computerized offices).

Supervise three Assistant Directors and fifteen management personnel.

Associate Director of Pricing. Inflight Division, 1/86-7/88.
Performed tasks listed below in addition to directing pricing for United States sales of approximately $200 million per year.

Assistant Director of International Pricing, Inflight Division, 5/83-1/86.
Monitored Sky Chef's inflight service throughout the world and traveled extensively with responsibility for audits, reviewing pricing procedures and making recommendations for menu changes/cost, service and delivery charges.

Supervised staff of cost analysts and consulted with airlines to recommend new menus and costs. Developed new formulas to accommodate evaluation and changing economy in Venezuela and Central America.

Reorganized price structure on all airlines supplied by Sky Chef in South America. Organized conversion of manual system to IBM computer system.

Marketing Liaison/Cost Analyst, Inflight Division, Miami,
Florida, 5/81-3/83.
  Served as liaison for Sky Chef to Eastern Airlines Headquarters
  Food Service in Miami. Monitored $100 million per year in sales
  from Eastern to Sky Chef; worked directly with airlines staff
  with emphasis on maintenance of menus and service in U.S. and
  South America.

  Negotiated new menu prices and service charges, authorized
  pricing structure and negotiated contracts with executive
  management.

Cost Analyst, Inflight Service, Dallas, Texas, 3/78-5/81.
  Responsible for costing menus and service charges for American,
  Braniff, Delta and Northwest Orient Airlines.

  Demonstrated frequent public relations skills while working
  with airline personnel. Performed field audits and
  negotiated cost and selling prices.

Office Manager, Internal Audit Department, 9/77-2/78.
  Supervised support staff, developed strategy to improve work
  flow, coordinated management questionnaire and maintained
  schedule of Sky Chef's audits and related reports.

Administrative Assistant to the Controller, Mid-Atlantic Region,
Inflight Service, Washington, D. C. National Airport, 9/76-8/77.
  Gathered statistical data for eight locations and completed
  reports for the Auto Train and Amtrak accounts.

Office Supervisor, Inflight Services, Boston, Massachusetts, 3-
8/76.
  Supervised office personnel and implemented a computer system
  for all airline billing.

Program Coordinator, Wishful Publishers, Wellesley,
Massachusetts, 5/74-2/76.
  Developed and monitored three yearly mailing campaigns and
  supervised all inventory/monthly cassette distribution.

Office Supervisor, Sky Chef Inflight Services, Boston,
Massachusetts, 8/73-4/74.
  Responsible for all payroll, personnel, accounts payable,
  airlines billing and inter/company statistical information.

EDUCATION:

B.A., English, Woburn College, Woburn, Massachusetts, 1973.
Secondary Education Teaching Certificate.

ADDITIONAL INFORMATION:

Worked with IBM Personal Computer and IBM System 34.

1. This is an overview of the work history. It should be a summary of the skills and accomplishments this individual can use to get another job.

2. This sentence would turn off prospective employers. It needs to be more generic.

3. This area is experience, not career highlights.

4. Eliminate months.

5. What is this?

6. Be consistent in layout and presentation. Inflight (Service? Division?) should be capitalized and identical throughout résumé. If all of these are Inflight, include the division below the organization's name.

STANLEY HUNT
16731 Harris Street
Dallas, Texas 75222

Home: (214) 556-6789
Work: (214) 789-0077

---

(1) OVERVIEW:

- Possess in-depth experience in management and finance for **(2)** Sky Chef Corporation.
- Adaptable to new and changing environments; traveled extensively throughout the United States, Europe and South America to analyze inflight food services.
- Successful in utilizing strong public relations skills in communicating with foreign business persons, colleagues and general public.
- Proficient writer in preparing documentation of foreign and domestic evaluations with a fluency in French.

(3) CAREER HIGHLIGHTS:

Sky Chef Corporation
Dallas, Texas
(4) August 1973-present

Director of Systems Support, 1988-present
 Direct all billing and computer applications for Inflight
(5) Catering Division (DEC: pricing, billing, inventory and requisitioning) with emphasis on coordinating all computer systems (main office computer tie-in to 60 satellite, computerized offices).

 Supervise three Assistant Directors and fifteen management personnel.
(6)

Associate Director of Pricing. Inflight Division, 1/86-7/88.
 Performed tasks listed below in addition to directing pricing for United States sales of approximately $200 million per year.

Assistant Director of International Pricing, Inflight Division, **(6)** 5/83-1/86.
(6) Monitored Sky Chef's inflight service throughout the world and traveled extensively with responsibility for audits, reviewing pricing procedures and making recommendations for menu changes/cost, service and delivery charges.

 Supervised staff of cost analysts and consulted with airlines to recommend new menus and costs. Developed new formulas to accommodate evaluation and changing economy in Venezuela and Central America.

 Reorganized price structure on all airlines supplied by Sky Chef in South America. Organized conversion of manual system to IBM computer system.

7. Too vague.

8. Why not delete these two positions? They don't add to the credentials. Either summarize or be prepared to discuss at the interview.

(6) Marketing Liaison/Cost Analyst, Inflight Division, Miami, Florida, 5/81-3/83.
  Served as liaison for Sky Chef to Eastern Airlines Headquarters Food Service in Miami. Monitored $100 million per year in sales from Eastern to Sky Chef; worked directly with airlines staff with emphasis on maintenance of menus and service in U.S. and South America.

  Negotiated new menu prices and service charges, authorized pricing structure and negotiated contracts with executive management.

(6) Cost Analyst, Inflight Service, Dallas, Texas, 3/78-5/81.
  Responsible for costing menus and service charges for American, Braniff, Delta and Northwest Orient Airlines.

(7) Demonstrated frequent public relations skills while working with airline personnel. Performed field audits and negotiated cost and selling prices.

Office Manager, Internal Audit Department, 9/77-2/78.
  Supervised support staff, developed strategy to improve work flow, coordinated management questionnaire and maintained schedule of Sky Chef's audits and related reports.

(6) Administrative Assistant to the Controller, Mid-Atlantic Region, Inflight Service, Washington, D. C. National Airport, 9/76-8/77.
  Gathered statistical data for eight locations and completed reports for the Auto Train and Amtrak accounts.

(6) Office Supervisor, Inflight Services, Boston, Massachusetts, 3-8/76.
  Supervised office personnel and implemented a computer system for all airline billing.

Program Coordinator, Wishful Publishers, Wellesley, Massachusetts, 5/74-2/76.
  Developed and monitored three yearly mailing campaigns and supervised all inventory/monthly cassette distribution.

(8)(6) Office Supervisor, Sky Chef Inflight Services, Boston, Massachusetts, 8/73-4/74.
  Responsible for all payroll, personnel, accounts payable, airlines billing and inter/company statistical information.

EDUCATION:

B.A., English, Woburn College, Woburn, Massachusetts, 1973.
Secondary Education Teaching Certificate.

ADDITIONAL INFORMATION:

Worked with IBM Personal Computer and IBM System 34.

Comments: Better organization is needed. A career summary would be effective but needs to highlight transferable skills/abilities.

STANLEY HUNT

16731 Harris Street, Dallas, Texas 75222

(214) 556-6789 (home)   (214) 789-0077 (work)

CAREER HISTORY

Successfully research and implement state-of-the-art technology to meet an organization's business needs. Ten years experience in financial analysis of airline catering; two years of international experience. Knowledge of Hispanic, French, British, Portuguese, and South African currency fluctuations, labor laws, and financial trends.

EXPERIENCE

SKY CHEF CORPORATION
Dallas, Texas
1973 - present

Director of Systems Support 1988 - present

Direct user group of eight expert managers. Research the latest technology and make recommendations to Information Systems Group. Oversee personal computer applications: establishment of Local Area Network, Wide Area Network for all satellite and Headquarters Network, and communication links.

Developed and implemented a three year plan: migrated existing programs from IBM to DEC environment for 60 satellite sites, set up new communication network, identified client needs, and provided electronic transfer of information.

Saved corporation $.5 million in long distance phone charges. Successfully negotiated contract with AT&T for best available long distance rates.

Associate Director of Pricing 1986 - 1988

Managed a staff of five Cost Analysts with revenue responsibility of $260 million. Directed the preparation of airline annual price actions and new business bids. Presented results of annual updates and bids to upper management and airline clients.

Successfully prepared bids netting $30 million in new business.

Merged Delta/Western and Northwestern/Republic pricing formulas to satisfaction of airline management.

Consistently achieved annual price action goals.

Assistant Director of International Pricing 1983-1986

Cost analysis consultant to international locations to ensure corporate objectives were met. Member of task force team that analyzed new venture opportunities.

Member of acquisition team in Paris and South Africa - netted organization $10 million in revenue.

Prepared numerous international bids for existing locations - awarded $3 million in contracts.

Taught pricing procedures and profit/loss analysis at several international locations.

Successfully returned Mexican facilities to a profitable position after inflation made pricing formulas obsolete. Negotiated new pricing formulas with airlines that are in use today.

Marketing Liaison/Cost Analyst 1981-1983

Provided on-site cost analysis for $100 million sales contract with Eastern Airlines. Negotiated weekly price variances with Eastern dining service management. Provided customers quality assurance in financial area. Maintained constantly changing menu specifications and service requirements for 40 domestic locations and five international locations.

Pioneered the installation and testing of electronic transfer of cost data.

Cost Analyst 1978-1981

Costed menus and service charges; developed preliminary analytical skills and obtained in-depth understanding of an industrial kitchen operation. Performed time and motion studies; established rapport with airline personnel.

1976 - 1978 Numerous administrative positions within the organization that provided understanding of field operations and developed analytical and computer skills.

EDUCATION

Bachelor of Arts, English (Secondary Teaching Certificate)
Woburn College, Woburn, Massachusetts, 1973

SKILLS

Use DEC MICROVAX Computers, IBM System 34
Lotus 1-2-3, dBASE IV, FreeLance, PageMaker, PS4

RYAN O'LEARY   15 Willow Lane, Boston, Massachusetts 02155   617/244-0900

MARKETING SPECIALIST

**SUMMARY OF
QUALIFICATIONS**   *M.B.A. in Marketing...Honor Society nominee...Strong experience in telephone services and related equipment sales...Successful performance of diverse administrative functions...Proven adeptness in human relations and problem solving...Equally adept in project liaison and coordination.*

EXPERIENCE

1979 - Present   **Service Representative, Massachusetts Bell, Boston, Massachusetts.**
Assigned to local business office with responsibility for variety of duties requiring one-on-one dealings with potential and current customers. Duties stress problem solving revolving around billing and service inquiries and complaints as well as settlement of customer disputes and misunderstandings. Also stress establishing service for new customers, handling transfers of service, and administering requests for telephone service installations, changes, and removals. Further stress answering correspondence from customers and selling telephone instruments and allied products. Have shown expertise on special projects such as flextime, interdepartmental awards and artwork. Also helped establish the training committee for the office. Selected for position at time of federal court-ordered breakup of AT&T. Prior to that was **Service Representative** at local **Phone Center Store** carrying out similar duties as in present position with additional responsibility for preparation of daily receipts deposits, maintenance of telephone displays and inventories, and initiating action requiring by evening mail and repair requests.

During this period attended Boston College from which received M.B.A. in Marketing in July 1983. Earned 3.8 Grade Point Average on 4.0 scale in 12 courses of three semester hours each. Based on "outstanding" academic record nominated for membership in Delta Kappa Chapter of Delta Epsilon Sigma National Honor Society. Studies focused on such courses as Marketing, Market Research, Advertising, Micro & Macro Economics, Personnel Management, and Production Management.

1978 - 1979   **Administrative Assistant, Howard Jones Incorporated, Boston, Massachusetts.** Responsible for multiple administrative duties for engineering/architectural firm acting under federal government contracts to determine costs of community flood insurance coverage at specific locations throughout the country. Entailed liaison with three other technical firms carrying out individual aspects of programs to coordinate their data with that of own company. Also entailed logging in and updating files-based on information provided by technical contractor - necessary for coordination and revision of emergency and regular flood insurance programs. Additionally responsible for drawing, revising, and computing costs of map compilation studies.

1977 - 1978   **Rental Agent, Hertz Rent-a-Car, Cambridge, Massachusetts** Performed all the duties involved in the renting and return of automobiles by travelers at Logan Airport. During same period also served as **Waitress, The Hungry Fisherman,** and **Desk Clerk, Ramada Inn.**

1974 - 1977   **Student, Boston College, Boston, Massachusetts.** Earned B.S. in Parks and Recreation Administration. Studies centered on such business courses as Management by Objectives, Economics, Finance, Statistics, and others which provided the prerequisites necessary for later matriculation for M.B.A. During same period served as **Recreation Coordinator, Land Between The Hills, Saugus, Massachusetts.** As such was responsible for programming and coordinating activities and special events for both modern group camp and family campground catering to church and Scout groups along with underprivileged and handicapped children and adults as well as the aged.

1970 - 1974   **Horse Trainer/Riding Instructor, Happy Hills Farms, Lowell, Massachusetts.** Prime responsibilities encompassed training and showing string of Morgan horses and providing riding instruction to people of all ages with varied experience and skill levels. During same period was **Assistant Manager/Sales Clerk, The Sloop, Lowell, Massachusetts,**involved in various management and sales activities of special apparel store. Also was **Student, Blair Junior College, Medford, Massachusetts,** where earned associate degree in Liberal Arts.

EDUCATION   M.B.A. Marketing, Boston College, Boston, Massachusetts, 1983.
B.S. Parks and Recreation, Boston College, Boston Massachusetts, 1977.
A.A. Liberal Arts, Blair Junior College, Medford, Massachusetts, 1973.

**VOLUNTEER
EXPERIENCE**   Junior Achievement - Volunteer Counselor, 1984; Reagan-Bush 1984 Presidential Campaign and Inauguration- Volunteer in the research department and administrative assistant; The Sporting Club of Boston - Nautilus instructor as a trade-out membership, 1985.

PERSONAL DATA   Born May 13, 1953; Single. Excellent health. Willing to travel. Salary negotiable. Immediately available.

REFERENCES   Available upon request.

1. This summary doesn't work—the information should add to the credentials. This information doesn't.

2. The type is so small, it can hardly be read.

3. This reads as if it was written in the third person. Too much duplication.

4. This is a separate position and should be written as such.

5. Include this information under education.

6. Too many words—consolidate.

7. Eliminate the waitress and desk clerk. It makes the résumé less professional.

8. Eliminate this.

9. Eliminate college work experiences once you have professional experience.

10. The A. A. degree can be eliminated.

RYAN O'LEARY   15 Willow Lane, Boston, Massachusetts 02155   617/244-0900

MARKETING SPECIALIST

SUMMARY OF QUALIFICATIONS ①

M.B.A. in Marketing...Honor Society nominee...Strong experience in telephone services and related equipment sales...Successful performance of diverse administrative functions...Proven adeptness in human relations and problem solving...Equally adept in project liaison and coordination.

EXPERIENCE

1979 - Present   **Service Representative, Massachusetts Bell, Boston, Massachusetts.** ②
Assigned to local business office with responsibility for variety of duties requiring one-on-one dealings with potential and current customers. Duties stress problem solving revolving around billing and service inquiries and complaints as well as settlement of customer disputes and misunderstandings. Also stress establishing service for new customers, handling transfers of service, and administering requests for telephone service installations, changes, and removals. Further stress answering correspondence from customers and selling telephone instruments and allied products. Have shown expertise on special projects such as flextime, interdepartmental awards and artwork. Also helped establish the training committee for the office. Selected for position at time of federal court-ordered breakup of AT&T. Prior to that was **Service Representative** at local **Phone Center Store** carrying out similar duties as in present position with additional responsibility for preparation of daily receipts deposits, maintenance of telephone displays and inventories, and initiating action requiring by evening mail and repair requests.

During this period attended Boston College from which received M.B.A. in Marketing in July 1983. Earned 3.8 Grade Point Average on 4.0 scale in 12 courses of three semester hours each. Based on "outstanding" academic record nominated for membership in Delta Kappa Chapter of Delta Epsilon Sigma National Honor Society. Studies focused on such courses as Marketing, Market Research, Advertising, Micro & Macro Economics, Personnel Management, and Production Management.

1978 - 1979   **Administrative Assistant, Howard Jones Incorporated, Boston, Massachusetts.** Responsible for multiple administrative duties for engineering/architectural firm acting under federal government contracts to determine costs of community flood insurance coverage at specific locations throughout the country. Entailed liaison with three other technical firms carrying out individual aspects of programs to coordinate their data with that of own company. Also entailed logging in and updating files-based on information provided by technical contractor - necessary for coordination and revision of emergency and regular flood insurance programs. Additionally responsible for drawing, revising, and computing costs of map compilation studies.

1977 - 1978   **Rental Agent, Hertz Rent-a-Car, Cambridge, Massachusetts** Performed all the duties involved in the renting and return of automobiles by travelers at Logan Airport. During same period also served as **Waitress, The Hungry Fisherman,** and **Desk Clerk, Ramada Inn.**

1974 - 1977   **Student, Boston College, Boston, Massachusetts.** Earned B.S. in Parks and Recreation Administration. Studies centered on such business courses as Management by Objectives, Economics, Finance, Statistics, and others which provided the prerequisites necessary for later matriculation for M.B.A. During same period served as **Recreation Coordinator, Land Between The Hills, Saugus, Massachusetts.** As such was responsible for programming and coordinating activities and special events for both modern group camp and family campground catering to church and Scout groups along with underprivileged and handicapped children and adults as well as the aged.

1970 - 1974   **Horse Trainer/Riding Instructor, Happy Hills Farms, Lowell, Massachusetts.** Prime responsibilities encompassed training and showing string of Morgan horses and providing riding instruction to people of all ages with varied experience and skill levels. During same period was **Assistant Manager/Sales Clerk, The Sloop, Lowell, Massachusetts,** involved in various management and sales activities of special apparel store. Also was **Student, Blair Junior College, Medford, Massachusetts,** where earned associate degree in Liberal Arts.

EDUCATION   M.B.A. Marketing, Boston College, Boston, Massachusetts, 1983.
B.S. Parks and Recreation, Boston College, Boston Massachusetts, 1977.
A.A. Liberal Arts, Blair Junior College, Medford, Massachusetts, 1973.

VOLUNTEER EXPERIENCE   Junior Achievement - Volunteer Counselor, 1984; Reagan-Bush 1984 Presidential Campaign and Inauguration- Volunteer in the research department and administrative assistant; The Sporting Club of Boston - Nautilus instructor as a trade-out membership, 1985.

PERSONAL DATA   Born May 13, 1953; Single. Excellent health. Willing to travel. Salary negotiable. Immediately available.

REFERENCES   Available upon request.

Comments: This résumé is far too crowded. A résumé shouldn't include every work experience you've had. Be selective and choose the experiences that indicate your qualifications.

RYAN O'LEARY
15 Willow Lane, Boston, Massachusetts 02155   617/244-0900

MARKETING SPECIALIST

EDUCATION

Boston College, Boston, Massachusetts
Masters in Business Administration, Marketing, 1983.
Earned 3.8 Grade Point Average. Nominated for membership in Delta Kappa Chapter of Delta Epsilon Sigma National Honor Society.
Bachelor of Science, Parks and Recreation 1977.

EXPERIENCE

Massachusetts Bell, Boston, Massachusetts

Customer Service Representative, **Residence Business Office, 1981-present**

Resolve customer inquiries, complaints, and billing errors utilizing effective problem solving techniques. Negotiate with customers to settle disputes and misunderstandings. Analyze and determine customer needs; coordinate transfers of service and requests for telephone service installations, changes, and removals. Review customer correspondence and initiate changes to resolve problems.

Direct responsibility for a variety of special projects from inception to completion: planned, researched, and presented final report on "Flextime Options", created interdepartmental awards and graphic designs for management seminars; established "Sales Quota Guide"; researched and produced "Student Guidebook for Telephone Service" and "Military Personnel Guidebook for Telephone Service."

Customer Service Representative, **Phone Center Store, 1979-1981**

Identifed and resolved customer service inquiries and problems. Marketed telephone equipment, maintained telephone displays and inventories, prepared daily receipts and deposits, and initiated action from repair requests. Supervised in absence of manager.

Howard Jones Incorporated, Washington, D. C.

Administrative Assistant, **1978-1979**

Handled administrative duties for engineering/architectural firm acting under federal government contracts to determine costs of community flood insurance coverage at specific locations throughout country. Coordinated information and ensured program compliance with three other technical firms carrying out individual aspects of program. Logged and updated files - based on information provided by technical contractor - necessary for coordination and revision of emergency and regular flood insurance programs. Drew, revised, and compulated costs of map compilation studies.

Hertz-Rent-A-Car, Cambridge, Massachusetts

Rental Agent, **1977-1978**

Performed all the duties involved in the rental and return of automobiles at Logan Airport.

VOLUNTEER EXPERIENCE

The Sporting Club - Nautilus Instructor, 1985-1987
Inauguration Volunteer in the research department and Administrative Assistant, 1985
Reagan-Bush Presidential Campaign, 1984
Junior Achievement- Volunteer Counselor, 1984

FRANK A. OLSON

1497 Green Meadow
Vienna, Virginia 22180

Home (703) 938-0081
Work (703) 889-5427

CAREER OBJECTIVE

Administrate or manage general training and specific areas such as Crisis Stress Management.

PROFESSIONAL EXPERIENCE

Town of Vienna Police Department 1967-present
Vienna, Virginia 22180

Master Police Officer III.

Fingerprint Computer Technician. Operate a $1.4 million state-of-the-art automated computer fingerprint system. Performed the benchmark testing and evaluation of the fingerprint computer system. Assisted in the planning and organization of a multi-jurisdictional fingerprint identification section comprised of ten police departments and a filing system of 125,000 fingerprint cards. Compile office production statistics. Senior officer responsible for the operation and supervision of personnel, for the past ten years, in the absence of the supervisor. Identify crime scene fingerprints and testify as a criminal court expert in the science of dactylography (fingerprints). Advisor and participant with the United States Bureau of Standards in the creation of a standard for the National Interchange of Fingerprint Identification Information and the standard for the benchmark testing of Automated Fingerprint Systems. Conduct training of investigators and patrol officers in the operation of an automated fingerprint system. Coordinate and assist outside agencies in the operation of the fingerprint computer system.

Senior Police Officer II.

Identification Officer. Senior officer in charge of the operation of the identification section in the absence of the supervisor. Preserve, process and collect evidence in serious crime scenes. Perform laboratory tests on crime scene evidence. Prepare and present court displays of crime scenes. Provide special graphics presentations for the office of the chief of police. Prepare work schedules for an eight man force. Worked in a darkroom developing and printing black and white photographs. Trained line supervisors, investigators, and patrol officers, in areas of crime scene preservation, fingerprinting, photography, criminal law and courtroom testimony.

Primary identification officer on the scene of the first mass murder in the history of Northern Virginia; the first tornado and the first highrise building collapse that killed 14 and injured 45 construction workers.

Produced video, 16mm movie and slide presentations on police related subjects. Talked to civic groups and individuals on the topics of home security and personal protection.

Juvenile Investigator. Handled cases of criminal child abuse, juvenile deliquency and crimes committed to and by juveniles. Provided guidance and assistance to troubled youngsters and their families.

58

Patrol Officer. Enforced traffic and criminal laws. Interceded in domestic disputes for the purpose of resolving potentially violent confrontations. Provided guidance and information to the public. Trained new officers in proper police techniques of report writing, accident investigation, criminal law enforcement and street survival. Prepared written evaluations to trainees.

United States Army 1965-1967
Military Police Specialist E-5. Performed building and operations surveys of military installations. Basic identification procedures, fingerprinting, photography, evidence collection. Investigated requests for financial support for military dependents. Protected dignitaries on visits to military facilities.

Federal Bureau of Investigation 1963-1965
Washington, D. C. 22070
Fingerprint Technician. Classified, searched and identified criminals, civilians and foreign nationals. Special assignment fingerprint searcher.
Tour guide. Provided an overview to thousands of visitors to the FBI Laboratories of their accomplishments towards crime solving.

EDUCATION

Georgetown University
Washington, D. C.
Bachelor of Science in The Administration of Justice 1974
Associates Degree in the Administration of Justice 1972

FORMAL TRAINING

Certified law enforcement instructor for the state of Virginia.

Criminal Investigation

Advanced Administrative Latent Fingerprint

Field Officer Trainer

Basic and Advanced Law Enforcement

SKILLS

Instructor for a year and a half with the Northern Virginia Community College, Manassas Campus, Manassas, Virginia.
Topic: Law Enforcement Photography

Professional photographer.

ORGANIZATIONS

Northern Virginia Chapter, United Ostomy Association.
Past Vice President
Treasurer
Directors Board
Fund Raising Chairman

Northern Virginia Chapter, Tandy Computer Users Group.

1. Too vague. Needs to be strengthened.

2. The dotted lines are hard on the eye.

3. Inconsistent shift in tense.

4. This is too sensational. As the individual is making a career change, this should be deemphasized.

5. Does this type of information support the career objective?

6. Paragraphs are too heavy.

FRANK A. OLSON

1497 Green Meadow   Home (703) 938-0081
Vienna, Virginia 22180   Work (703) 889-5427

----

(2)

CAREER OBJECTIVE

(1)

     Administrate or manage general training and specific areas such as Crisis Stress Management.

PROFESSIONAL EXPERIENCE

Town of Vienna Police Department 1967-present
Vienna, Virginia 22180
    Master Police Officer III.
    <u>Fingerprint Computer Technician.</u> Operatea $1.4 million state-of-the-art automated computer fingerprint system. Performed the benchmark testing and evaluation of the fingerprint computer system. Assisted in the planning and organization of a multi-jurisdictional fingerprint identification section comprised of ten police departments and a filing system of 125,000 fingerprint cards. Compile office production statistics. Senior officer responsible for the operation and supervision of personnel, for the past ten years, in the absence of the supervisor. Identify crime scene fingerprints and testify as a criminal court expert in the science of dactylography (fingerprints). Advisor and participant with the United States Bureau of Standards in the creation of a standard for the National Interchange of Fingerprint Identification Information and the standard for the benchmark testing of Automated Fingerprint Systems. Conduct training of investigators and patrol officers in the operation of an automated fingerprint system. Coordinate and assist outside agencies in the operation of the fingerprint computer system.

(3)

(6)

    Senior Police Officer II.
    <u>Identification Officer.</u> Senior officer in charge of the operation of the identification section in the absence of the supervisor. Preserve, process and collect evidence in serious crime scenes. Perform laboratory tests on crime scene evidence. Prepare and present court displays of crime scenes. Provide special graphics presentations for the office of the chief of police. Prepare work schedules for an eight man force. Worked in a darkroom developing and printing black and white photographs. Trained line supervisors, investigators, and patrol officers, in areas of crime scene preservation, fingerprinting, photography, criminal law and courtroom testimony.
    Primary identification officer on the scene of the first mass murder in the history of Northern Virginia; the first tornado and the first highrise building collapse that killed 14 and injured 45 construction workers.
    Produced video, 16mm movie and slide presentations on police related subjects. Talked to civic groups and individuals on the topics of home security and personal protection.

(4)

(5)

    <u>Juvenile Investigator.</u> Handled cases of criminal child abuse, juvenile deliquency and crimes committed to and by juveniles. Provided guidance and assistance to troubled youngsters and their families.

7. Omit.

8. The degree is Associate in Applied Science.

9. Where did this training take place?

(7)   <u>Patrol Officer.</u> Enforced traffic and criminal laws. Interceded in domestic disputes for the purpose of resolving potentially violent confrontations. Provided guidance and information to the public. Trained new officers in proper police techniques of report writing, accident investigation, criminal law enforcement and street survival. Prepared written evaluations to trainees.

United States Army 1965-1967
<u>Military Police Specialist E-5.</u> Performed building and operations surveys of military installations. Basic identification procedures, fingerprinting, photography, evidence collection. Investigated requests for financial support for military dependents. Protected dignitaries on visits to military facilities.

Federal Bureau of Investigation 1963-1965
Washington, D. C. 22070
<u>Fingerprint Technician.</u> Classified, searched and identified criminals, civilians and foreign nationals. Special assignment fingerprint searcher.
<u>Tour guide.</u> Provided an overview to thousands of visitors to the FBI Laboratories of their accomplishments towards crime solving.

EDUCATION

Georgetown University
Washington, D. C.
Bachelor of Science in The Administration of Justice 1974
(8) Associates Degree in the Administration of Justice 1972

FORMAL TRAINING

Certified law enforcement instructor for the state of Virginia.

Criminal Investigation

(9) Advanced Administrative Latent Fingerprint

Field Officer Trainer

Basic and Advanced Law Enforcement

SKILLS

Instructor for a year and a half with the Northern Virginia Community College, Manassas Campus, Manassas, Virginia.
Topic: Law Enforcement Photography

Professional photographer.

ORGANIZATIONS

Northern Virginia Chapter, United Ostomy Association.
Past Vice President
Treasurer
Directors Board
Fund Raising Chairman

Northern Virginia Chapter, Tandy Computer Users Group.

Comments: While this individual has had increased responsibility, a chronological résumé does not work for a change to a training position. The résumé as it exists highlights police work. There have been many training experiences and these need to be emphasized. A recruiter will not hunt for them.

Frank A. Olson

1497 Green Meadow, Vienna, Virginia 22180   (h) 703/938-0081   (w) 703/889-5427

Career Objective

A position as a training specialist in private industry working with staff development.

---

10 years of training experience in all aspects of police operation:

- Conduct training programs for investigators and patrol officers in the operation of an automated fingerprint system.
- Train line supervisors, investigators, and patrol officers in crime scene preservation, fingerprinting, photography, criminal law, and courtroom testimony.
- Produce video, 16mm movie, and slide presentations on crime scene preservation and fingerprinting.
- Prepare and present speeches on home security and personal protection to civic groups and individuals.
- Train new officers in proper police techniques of report writing, accident investigation, criminal law enforcement, and street survival.
- Taught Law Enforcement Photography at local community college.

20 years of increased responsibility with the Town of Vienna Police Department:

- Manage a 1.4 million state-of-the-art automated computer fingerprint system.
- Specialist in crime scene fingerprint identification and testify as criminal court expert in the science of dactylography (fingerprints).
- Manage the operation and supervision of 65 police officers in absence of supervisor.
- Assist in the planning and organization for a multi-jurisdictional fingerprint identification section comprised of ten police departments and a filing system of 125,000 fingerprint cards.
- Perform the benchmark testing and evaluation of the fingerprint computer system.
- Advisor and participant with the United States Bureau of Standards in creation of a standard for the National Interchange of Fingerprint Identification Information and the standard for the benchmark testing of Automated Fingerprint Systems.

Education and Certification:

Georgetown University, Washington, D.C.
  Bachelor of Science in The Administration of Justice, 1974.
  Associate in Applied Science in The Administration of Justice, 1972.

Fairfax County Criminal Justice Academy, Fairfax, Virginia.
  Criminal Investigation, Advanced Administrative Latent Fingerprint, Field Officer Training, Basic and Advanced Law Enforcement.

Certified Law Enforcement Instructor for the state of Virginia.

Professional Organizations:

United Ostomy Association, Northern Virginia Chapter.
  Past Vice-President, Treasurer, Board of Directors, Fund Raising Chairman.

Tandy Computer Users Group, Northern Virginia Chapter.

MARG GRADY SMITH

100 Maple Street
Fairfax, Virginia 22013
Home: (703) 255-0001
Work: (703) 234-0908

CAREER OBJECTIVE

Position utilizing experience as an international economist and country
risk analyst in export-oriented company.

PROFESSIONAL EXPERIENCE

FINANCIAL ECONOMIST   1979 to present
United States Bank
Washington, D. C.
> --analyzes and monitors economic and political developments in
>   23 West African countries.
> --develops balance of payments and external debt forecasts for
>   major West African markets.
> --provides policy recommendations to senior management on country
>   creditworthiness with respect to new United States Bank exposure.
> --briefs United States Bank senior management, U. S. Government
>   and foreign government officials, exporters, and bankers on
>   United States Bank country policies.
> --coordinates United States Bank lending policies in West Africa
>   with other U. S. Government agencies.
> --initiates and pursues collection efforts in cases of overdue
>   payments resulting from country economic problems.
> --assesses general techniques and standards of United States Bank
>   country risk analysis as part of economists' task force.

INTERNATIONAL ECONOMIST   1978-79
United States Government
Washington, D. C.
> --coordinated interagency actions to reduce foreign debt
>   arrears.
> --prepared briefing material for Congressional hearings on
>   on foreign debt owed to the U. S. Government.
> --researched issues in developing countries' finance in
>   particular external indebtedness, debt reschedulings, and the
>   stabilization of export earnings.
> --provided briefing materials for senior Treasury officials
>   and U. S. delegations on developing finance issues.
> --submitted quarterly reports to Congress on debt arrears and
>   answered Congressional correspondence and letters from the
>   public on this subject.

EDUCATION

UNIVERSITY OF VIRGINIA, Charlottesville, Virginia
        Advanced graduate studies in international economics and
        foreign affairs, Governor's Fellowship, 1976-78.
FLETCHER SCHOOL OF LAW AND DIPLOMACY, Tufts University, Medford,
        Massachusetts.
        Master of Arts in international relations, 1975.
DUKE UNIVERSITY, Durham, North Carolina.
        Bachelor of Arts in French, magna cum laude, 1974.
        Study abroad: University of Nice, France and Oxford University,
        England.

HONORS

Listing in Who's Who of American Women
United States Bank Outstanding Performance Award--1981, 1984, 1986
United States Bank Special Achievement Award--1982, 1985

PERSONAL

Born: June 11, 1946
Marital Status: Divorced
Children: 3
Health: Excellent

1. The heading takes up too much space—almost 25% of the page.

2. This sounds self serving—what can you offer the organization? Not what they can offer you!

3. Dates are hanging.

4. Responsibilities of current position should be in present tense—do not add an "s" to verbs.

5. Awkward sentence. Poor word choice.

6. This clarification adds extra words and some awkwardness— omit.

7. Typo—"on" appears twice.

8. Dashes are not visually appealing.

9. Too much white space.

10. Headings are the same type— one doesn't stand out from the other.

MARG GRADY SMITH

100 Maple Street
Fairfax, Virginia 22013
Home: (703) 255-0001
Work: (703) 234-0908

CAREER OBJECTIVE

(2) Position utilizing experience as an international economist and country risk analyst in export-oriented company.

(10) PROFESSIONAL EXPERIENCE

FINANCIAL ECONOMIST   1979 to present (3)
United States Bank
Washington, D. C.

--analyzes and monitors economic and political developments in 23 West African countries.
--develops balance of payments and external debt forecasts for major West African markets.
(4) --provides policy recommendations to senior management on country creditworthiness with respect to new United States Bank exposure.
--briefs United States Bank senior management, U. S. Government and foreign government officials, exporters, and bankers on United States Bank country policies.
--coordinates United States Bank lending policies in West Africa with other U. S. Government agencies.
--initiates and pursues collection efforts in cases of overdue payments resulting from country economic problems.
--assesses general techniques and standards of United States Bank country risk analysis as part of economists' task force.

INTERNATIONAL ECONOMIST   1978-79
United States Government
Washington, D. C.

(5) --coordinated interagency actions to reduce foreign debt arrears.
--prepared briefing material for Congressional hearings on (7) on foreign debt owed to the U. S. Government.
--researched issues in developing countries' finance in particular external indebtedness, debt reschedulings, and the stabilization of export earnings.
(8) --provided briefing materials for senior Treasury officials and U. S. delegations on developing finance issues.
--submitted quarterly reports to Congress on debt arrears and answered Congressional correspondence and letters from the public on this subject.

11. The schools are too large and overshadow the degrees.

12. Too much white space.

13. The personal data do not add to the qualifications of the individual or make her a more desirable candidate.

(12)

EDUCATION

UNIVERSITY OF VIRGINIA, Charlottesville, Virginia
        Advanced graduate studies in international economics and
        foreign affairs, Governor's Fellowship, 1976-78.

(11) FLETCHER SCHOOL OF LAW AND DIPLOMACY, Tufts University, Medford,
        Massachusetts.
        Master of Arts in international relations, 1975.

DUKE UNIVERSITY, Durham, North Carolina.
        Bachelor of Arts in French, magna cum laude, 1974.
        Study abroad: University of Nice, France and Oxford University,
        England.

HONORS

Listing in Who's Who of American Women
United States Bank Outstanding Performance Award--1981, 1984, 1986
United States Bank Special Achievement Award--1982, 1985

PERSONAL

(13)

Born: June 11, 1946
Marital Status: Divorced
Children: 3
Health: Excellent

Comments: Two pages aren't necessary. The résumé should be reworded and formatted to fit on one page. Too much overall white space. Try bullets (•) instead of dashes (--).

MARG G. SMITH
100 Maple Avenue
Fairfax, Virginia 22013

Home: (703) 255-0001
Work: (703) 234-0908

Career Objective: A position requiring expertise as an international economist and country risk analyst in an export oriented organization.

PROFESSIONAL EXPERIENCE

Financial Economist, United States Bank, Washington, D. C.
1979 - present

- Analyze and monitor economic and political developments in 23 West African countries.
- Develop balance of payments and external debt forecasts for major West African markets.
- Conduct country risk analysis and provide recommendations to senior management for new loans.
- Brief bank senior management, United States Government and foreign government officials, exporters, and bankers on bank policies.
- Coordinate lending policies in West Africa with other United States government agencies.
- Initiate and pursue collection activities for overdue payments resulting from a country's economic difficulties.
- Assess general techniques and standards of bank country risk analysis as member of Economic Task Force.

International Economist, United States Government, Washington, D. C.
1978 - 1979

- Coordinated interagency actions to reduce overdue payments on foreign debt.
- Researched developing countries' finances including external indebtedness, stabilization of export earnings and debt reschedulings.
- Prepared and provided briefing material for Congressional hearings on foreign debt owed to United States government and to senior government officials and United States delegations on developing finance issues.
- Submitted quarterly reports to Congress on delinquent loans and answered Congressional correspondence and letters from the public.

EDUCATION

University of Virginia, Charlottesville, Virginia.
Advanced graduate studies in international economics and foreign affairs.
Governor's Fellowship, 1976 - 1978.

Fletcher School of Law and Diplomacy, Tufts University, Medford, Massachusetts.
Master of Arts in international relations, 1975.

Duke University, Durham, North Carolina.
Bachelor of Arts in French, magna cum laude, 1974.

HONORS

United States Bank Outstanding Performance Award, 1981, 1984, 1986
United States Bank Special Achievement Award, 1982, 1985
Listing in Who's Who of American Women

67

RESUME
OF
LAURA CURTIN

Address: 290 Park Avenue
                 Williamstown, Virginia 22456
Telephone: (703) 450-0090
Date of Birth: January 6, 1952
Martial Status: Single

PROFESSIONAL EXPERIENCE

Marketing: Proficient in strategic planning on both the corporate
                 and private industry segment; long term as well as short
                 term goal targeting. Skilled in research, analysis, pro-
                 duct and industry segment projections, report computation,
                 and corporate orientation. Demonstrable talents in eval-
                 uation and forecasting of technological innovation, en-
                 vironmental and socio-economic transgressions. Developed
                 analytical framework for analysis of various industries,
                 determining growth potential through acquisitions, mergers,
                 and technical expansion. Conducted market research in all
                 phases of analysis in numerous areas, including problem and
                 objective identification, market survey design, results
                 evaluation, development of planning documents, goal formation,
                 promotional campaign design, and implementation.

Administration: Developed optimal scheduling to increase staff effectiveness.
                 Redesigned training program of staff resulting in increased
                 longevity. Analyzed maintenance necessities and developed
                 a schedule to routinely prevent problems.

Management: Contacted local administration to broaden employee base.
                 Effective and conscientious management resulting in 19%
                 increase in sales. Trained future managers. Maintained
                 and managed entire product line, as well as developed and
                 displayed "theme" products. Rapid comprehension and know-
                 ledge of product, coupled with selling ability propelled
                 standings to highest in Eastern region. Maintained strict
                 accountability of inventory to a 1 % or less variance
                 against a separate accounting system.

PROFESSIONAL POSITIONS

Partner, Curtin, Smith and Brams	1986
Manager, The Horseshoe Restaurant	1983-1985
Manager, Roy Ralwings Restaurant	1982
Manager, F and R Restaurant	1980-1982
Cosmetic Representative, Revlon Cosmetics	1976-1979

EDUCATION   Master of Business Administration in Marketing, George
                 Mason University, Fairfax, Virginia. December 1986.

                 Bachelor of Arts in English, South Hampton College, Long
                 Island, New York. June 1975.

PROFESSIONAL   American Marketing Association
AFFILIATIONS   George Mason Alumni Association

1. Don't waste space writing "résumé"—It's obvious it is a résumé.

2. Eliminate personal information. Ask yourself, "Does this make me more qualified for this position?"

3. Incorrect punctuation. These are separate sentences.

4. Incorrect punctuation.

5. Use colon here.

6. "Prepared" or "planned" are better word choices.

7. Awkward sentences. What do they mean? What are you trying to say?

8. "Work History" sounds better.

9. Eliminate the month.

10. Does this add to your qualifications? Omit "Alumni Association" unless you are an officer.

11. Placing school and degree on same line doesn't highlight either. Use separate lines and underline or boldface one of them.

12. Too much white space.

13. Shift in tense.

14. "Tenure" is a better word choice.

15. Paragraphs are too long and difficult to read.

---

(1) RESUME
OF
LAURA CURTIN

Address: 290 Park Avenue
                    Williamstown, Virginia 22456
Telephone: (703) 450-0090
Date of Birth: January 6, 1952 (2)
Martial Status: Single

PROFESSIONAL EXPERIENCE (3)

Marketing: Proficient in strategic planning on both the corporate and private industry segment; long term as well as short term goal targeting. Skilled in research, analysis, product and industry segment projections, report computation, (15) and corporate orientation. Demonstrable talents in evaluation and forecasting of technological innovation, environmental and socio-economic transgressions. Developed analytical framework for analysis of various industries, determining growth potential through acquisitions, mergers, and technical expansion. Conducted market research in all (5) phases of analysis in numerous areas, including problem and (4) objective identification, market survey design, results evaluation, development of planning documents, goal formation, promotional campaign design, and implementation.

Administration: Developed optimal scheduling to increase staff effectiveness. Redesigned training program of staff resulting in increased (14) longevity. Analyzed maintenance necessities and developed (6) a schedule to routinely prevent problems.

Management: Contacted local administration to broaden employee base. (13) Effective and conscientious management resulting in 19% increase in sales. Trained future managers. Maintained and managed entire product line, as well as developed and (7) displayed "theme" products. Rapid comprehension and knowledge of product, coupled with selling ability propelled (12) standings to highest in Eastern region. Maintained strict accountability of inventory to a 1 % or less variance against a separate accounting system.

(8) PROFESSIONAL POSITIONS

<u>Partner,</u> Curtin, Smith and Brams   1986
<u>Manager,</u> The Horseshoe Restaurant   1983-1985
<u>Manager,</u> Roy Ralwings Restaurant   1982
<u>Manager,</u> F and R Restaurant   1980-1982
<u>Cosmetic Representative,</u> Revlon Cosmetics 1976-1979

EDUCATION (11)   Master of Business Administration in Marketing, George Mason University, Fairfax, Virginia. December 1986. (9)

                    Bachelor of Arts in English, South Hampton College, Long Island, New York. June 1975.

PROFESSIONAL   American Marketing Association
AFFILIATIONS   George Mason Alumni Association (10)

Comments: Nothing on this résumé stands out and it lacks eye appeal. Paragraphs are too heavy. Word choice is often clumsy and stilted.

LAURA CURTIN

290 Park Avenue
Williamstown, Virginia 22456

703/450-0090 (h)
703/450-2600 (w)

CAREER OBJECTIVE

A position offering opportunity to demonstrate abilities and advance in the field of product planning and research.

CAPABILITIES AND RELATED ACCOMPLISHMENTS

Marketing. Developed and implemented market research program for client which resulted in sales increasing 50 percent over prior year.

—Observed client operations
—Identified customer tastes
—Drafted and administered questionnaire
—Designed sample for study

—Trained interviewers
—Developed software for program
—Drafted analysis plan
—Prepared report and made final recommendations

Management. Operated a number of fast food restaurants and supervised staffs of up to 30 persons.

—Hired and trained staff
—Developed recruiting program
—Trained shift managers and other supervisors
—Resolved problems requiring immediate action before opening

—Created system to highlight employee skills and improve morale
—Established incentive programs to increase productivity
—Evaluated employee progress and reviewed performance
—Worked with accounting and local advertising consultants

Planning and Control. Initiated six and twelve month planning cycles to move new facilities from a negative to a positive profit status. Operated 19 percent ahead of profits estimated by franchise firm.

—Established inventory control and minimum lead time for purchases
—Implemented daily fiscal reports to quickly spot problem areas

—Broke sales forecasts down by product to identify areas requiring marketing support
—Informed banker of our progress and obtained refinancing of loan at more favorable rate

EDUCATION

Master of Business Administration (Marketing). George Mason University, Fairfax Virginia, 1986
Bachelor of Arts (English), South Hampton College, Montauk, New York, 1975

Suzanne Fine
12 Park Avenue
New York, NY 12202

Home: 765-5432

EXPERIENCE: MASON TEXTILES, NEW YORK, NEW YORK 12234
December, 1986-present
Assistant Controller for a textile firm with large
volume of sales. Work involves preparing budgets
and financial statements and analyzing payables and
receivables. Handle a variety of audit work.
Experienced in the areas of federal sales tax
returns and bank reconciliations. Supervise
employees.

OPTIC FIBERS, NEW YORK, NEW YORK 12312
June, 1984-November, 1986
Chief Accountant for a fiber manufacturer.
Responsible for cashier and payroll departments and
three clerks.

June, 1982-June, 1984
Staff Accountant. Experienced in coordinating and
auditing payroll. Direct involvement in the conversion to an automated payroll system. Filed
payroll tax returns.

METRO BOOKKEEPING SERVICE, NEW YORK, NEW YORK 12315
May, 1981-May, 1982

Part-time assistant to bookkeeper while in college.
Handled a variety of duties as needed.

EDUCATION: B.S. Hunter College, 1982. Successfully passed the
CPA exam.

PROFESSIONAL   Member of the American Institute of Certified
AFFILIATIONS: Public Accountants and National Association of
Accountants.

1. This shouldn't be all capitals. Include only organization name, city, and state. Exclude the zip code.

2. What type of volume? Quantify here.

3. What kind of audit work? Expand here.

4. How many employees? Be specific.

5. Job titles are lost. Highlight them.

6. What exactly was done? This is too vague and needs expansion.

7. I would delete this position. There is enough solid work experience after college. You would only include this experience if you were a recent college graduate who needed more experience.

8. This should be listed separately under "Licenses." I would also add CPA after the name. This is an accomplishment and should be highlighted right at the beginning.

9. Bachelor of Science in what? Where is the school located? Include city and state.

Suzanne Fine
12 Park Avenue
New York, NY 12202

Home: 765-5432

EXPERIENCE: MASON TEXTILES, NEW YORK, NEW YORK 12234 (1)
December, 1986-present
(5)
(2)   Assistant Controller for a textile firm with large volume of sales. Work involves preparing budgets and financial statements and analyzing payables and receivables. Handle a variety of audit work. (3) Experienced in the areas of federal sales tax returns and bank reconciliations. Supervise employees. (4)

OPTIC FIBERS, NEW YORK, NEW YORK 12312
June, 1984-November, 1986
(5)   Chief Accountant for a fiber manufacturer. Responsible for cashier and payroll departments and (6) three clerks.

June, 1982-June, 1984
(5)   Staff Accountant. Experienced in coordinating and auditing payroll. Direct involvement in the conversion to an automated payroll system. Filed payroll tax returns.

METRO BOOKKEEPING SERVICE, NEW YORK, NEW YORK 12315
May, 1981-May, 1982

(7)   Part-time assistant to bookkeeper while in college. Handled a variety of duties as needed.

EDUCATION: (9)   B.S. Hunter College, 1982. Successfully passed the CPA exam. (8)

PROFESSIONAL
AFFILIATIONS: Member of the American Institute of Certified Public Accountants and National Association of Accountants.

Comments Résumé is dull. It lacks accomplishments and the responsibilities are vague. Experience areas need to be expanded and written in the active voice. How about a career objective?

SUZANNE FINE CPA

12 Park Avenue, New York, New York 12202 (212) 765-5432 (h) (212) 765-8989 (w)

CAREER OBJECTIVE
A challenging position as a controller in private industry.

EXPERIENCE

Mason Textiles, New York, New York

1986-present **Assistant Controller**

Accounting and administrative responsibility for organization with $26 million in sales. Prepare budgets and financial statements, analyze payables and receivables. Audit employee and sub-contractor payroll, state and federal sales tax returns, export documents, and bank reconciliations. Manage staff of six; recruit, supervise, train, and appraise performance.

Implemented credit and collection program that reduced receivables by 30%. Recommended changes in valuation of assets that reduced cost of insurance by 15%.

Optic Fibers, New York, New York

1984 - 1986 **Chief Accountant**

Supervised and coordinated cashier and payroll departments for organization with $11 million in sales. Managed staff of three. Streamlined payroll process; reduced administrative overhead, saved organization $125,000, and received bonus.

1982 - 1984 **Staff Accountant**

Coordinated and audited payroll for 100 employees. Oversaw conversion to automated payroll system, revised procedures, and prepared federal and state payroll tax returns. Supervised staff of two.

EDUCATION Hunter College, New York, New York
Bachelor of Science in Accounting, 1982

LICENSES Certified Public Accountant

PROFESSIONAL ASSOCIATIONS American Institute of Certified Public Accountants
National Association of Accountants

73

ROBERT LANE

54 Broad Street
Fort Wayne, IN 46802

home (219) 422-1000
work (219) 423-3000

BACKGROUND SUMMARY

Over twenty years experience as an internal and external consultant to businesses including four years with one of the largest professional firms in the world. Direction, problem solving and project management in the operational, financial and administrative functions. Additional expertise in the development and marketing of consulting services. An established ability to develop, communicate and implement practical and effective solutions at various levels of both major corporations and small businesses.

EDUCATION

MBA, Marketing
School of Business Administration, Indiana State University, Fort Wayne, Indiana

BS, Marketing/Data Processing
University of Indiana, South Bend, Indiana

PROFESSIONAL EXPERIENCE

Lane and Associates
President 1984 to present
Responsible for developing human resource programs and clients for human resource consulting firm. Participated directly in the development of marketing plans and strategies. The major areas of emphasis include:

- Market analysis and planning
- Service development
- Strategic planning
- Marketing communications
- Program delivery

Touche Ross
Manager 1980 to 1984
Senior Consultant 1977 to 1980
Consulted with a variety of client organizations, ranging in size from Fortune 500 companies to start up businesses. Worked with client executives at the CEO, the CFO, the functional head and supervisor levels. Directed Touche Ross and client technical, professional, managerial, supervisory and clerical staff. The major areas of consulting emphasis include:

- Strategic, tactical and operational planning
- Organizational structure
- Product development and marketing
- Management information systems requirements
- Work measurement and manpower program development
- Operations reviews
- Project management

Indiana Savings Bank
  Operations Officer, 1974 to 1977
  Senior Analyst, 1972 to 1974
  Junior Analyst, 1970 to 1972
    Participated in diversified internal consulting projects. As group manager, participated on senior project teams to develop overall business strategies. Supervised a staff of 7 professionals and 3 clerical personnel. The major areas of consulting emphasis include:

- Work measurement and manpower management
- Operations improvement
- Cash management
- Automated systems implementation
- Project management

PROFESSIONAL ASSOCIATIONS

Member, International Association of Consultants
Member, Human Resources Management Society
Member, Banking Managers Association
Member, Association of Human Resource Consultants
Past Treasurer, North American MOHUMNS Association

1. The impact of an effective summary is lost when it is too long. Choose only the most pertinent information.

2. Place after experience. Why are the dates not included?

3. Listing responsibilities is ineffective. What was accomplished?

4. Don't abbreviate. This can be expressed as ''worked with all levels of management.''

5. Use the past tense for all past experiences.

6. Too much white space.

ROBERT LANE

54 Broad Street
Fort Wayne, IN 46802

home (219) 422-1000
work (219) 423-3000

(1) BACKGROUND SUMMARY

Over twenty years experience as an internal and external consultant to businesses including four years with one of the largest professional firms in the world. Direction, problem solving and project management in the operational, financial and administrative functions. Additional expertise in the development and marketing of consulting services. An established ability to develop, communicate and implement practical and effective solutions at various levels of both major corporations and small businesses.

(2) EDUCATION

MBA, Marketing
School of Business Administration, Indiana State University, Fort Wayne, Indiana

BS, Marketing/Data Processing
University of Indiana, South Bend, Indiana

PROFESSIONAL EXPERIENCE (6)

Lane and Associates
  President 1984 to present
  Responsible for developing human resource programs and clients for human resource consulting firm. Participated directly in the development of marketing plans and strategies. The major areas of emphasis include:

(3)
  • Market analysis and planning
  • Service development
  • Strategic planning
  • Marketing communications
  • Program delivery

Touche Ross
  Manager 1980 to 1984
  Senior Consultant 1977 to 1980
  Consulted with a variety of client organizations, ranging in size from Fortune 500 companies to start up businesses. Worked with client executives at the CEO, the CFO, the functional head and supervisor levels. Directed Touche Ross and client technical, professional, managerial, supervisory and clerical staff. The major areas of consulting emphasis include: (5) (4)

(3)
  • Strategic, tactical and operational planning
  • Organizational structure
  • Product development and marketing
  • Management information systems requirements
  • Work measurement and manpower program development
  • Operations reviews
  • Project management

7. What does this mean?

8. What is this?

9. Eliminate the word ''member.''

Indiana Savings Bank
  Operations Officer, 1974 to 1977
  Senior Analyst, 1972 to 1974
  Junior Analyst, 1970 to 1972
    Participated in diversified internal consulting projects. As group manager, participated on senior project teams to develop overall business strategies. Supervised a staff of 7 professionals and 3 clerical personnel. The major areas of consulting emphasis include: **(5)** **(7)**

- Work measurement and manpower management
- Operations improvement
- Cash management
- Automated systems implementation
- Project management

PROFESSIONAL ASSOCIATIONS

(9)
Member, International Association of Consultants
Member, Human Resources Management Society
Member, Banking Managers Association
Member, Association of Human Resource Consultants
Past Treasurer, North American MOHUMNS Association
(8)

Comments: Far too much white space. This needs to be rewritten so that it shows the steady career progression. It can fit on one page.

ROBERT LANE
54 BROAD STREET, FORT WAYNE, INDIANA 46802
(219) 422-1000 (H) (219) 423-3000 (W)

MANAGEMENT CONSULTANT

QUALIFICATIONS SUMMARY

20 years of progressive experience in the areas of human resources, financial management, recruiting, training, organizational development, and systems acquisition.

EXPERIENCE

1984 - PRESENT   **Lane and Associates**
                                                                  Fort Wayne, Indiana

President of human resource consulting firm. Perform management consultant tasks for clients in the public and private sectors; design and implement recruitment, employee retention, and training programs.

1977 - 1984   **Touche Ross**
                                                                  Fort Wayne, Indiana

Promoted from Senior Consultant to Manager of Financial Support Services division. Directed a staff of 50 to provide marketing, product development, and management information systems to clients ranging from Fortune 500 to start-up businesses. Worked with all levels of management. Increased scope of work and demonstrated ability to deliver superior products and services. Division growth consistently exceeded targets by 15% under my leadership.

1969 - 1977   **Indiana Savings Bank**
                                                                  Fort Wayne, Indiana

Promoted three times to increasingly responsible positions. As Operations Officer, participated in diversified consulting projects to develop overall business strategies. Directed the efforts of a ten member team of seven professionals and three clericals. Initiated and implemented programs to attract corporate and small business clients. Increased new business by $1 million.

EDUCATION

Masters in Business Administration, Marketing
   Indiana State University, Fort Wayne, Indiana, 1980
Bachelor of Science, Marketing/Data Processing
   University of Indiana, South Bend, Indiana, 1970

PROFESSIONAL ASSOCIATIONS

International Association of Consultants
Human Resource Management Society
Banking Managers Association
Association of Human Resource Consultants

PAMELA AUBREY
18 Oakley Avenue, Pittsburgh, Pennsylvania 15222
(412) 766-9222(b)   (412) 755-4444 (h)

PROFESSIONAL OBJECTIVE
Senior general management position utilizing extensive sales/marketing expertise in a major organization.

PROFESSIONAL EXPERIENCE

REGION MANAGER   1980 - present
IBM Corporation
Pittsburgh, Pennsylvania
(eight branches)
○ Sales Revenue - $400M annually
○ 2,500 employees (Sales, Service and Administration)
○ #1 NEWS (National Employment Work Survey) Region
○ #1 Service Region
○ #1 Response Time Region
○ Developed an Employee Involvement Program

REGION MANAGER   1978 - 1980
IBM Corporation
Columbus, Ohio
(six branches)
○ Sales Revenue - $280M annually
○ 1,300 employees
○ #1-in 1979 and 1980

MANAGER, GEM   1976 - 1978
(GOVERNMENT, EDUCATION AND
MEDICAL MARKETING)
IBM Corporation
Stamford, Connecticut
○ 4 employees - staff assignment
○ Responsible for development and implementation of marketing
  strategies (pricing, advertising, compensation, etc.) for the
  State, Local, and Federal Government, Education and Medical
  markets.

BRANCH MANAGER I   1973 - 1976
IBM Corporation
Hartford, Connecticut
○ Sales Revenue - $40M nationally
○ 290 employees
○ Brought Hartford Branch from 82nd to 1st in Branch Rankings,
  finishing #2 nationally in Sales and #4 in overall performance.
  Increased revenues from 27.0 million dollars to approximately
  40.0 million dollars in four years of management

79

SALES MANAGER   1971 - 1973
IBM Corporation
Hartford, Connecticut
○ Six Sales Representatives
○ Fifteen million dollars in revenue
○ #1 Sales Manager in region
○ Youngest sales manager in branch history

SALES REPRESENTATIVE   1969 - 1971
IBM Corporation
Hartford, Connecticut
○ Managed territory of 1,000 customers
○ Top ranking sales rep in 1971
○ #1 sales rep in New England region in 1970

EDUCATION

1973   Yale University   MBA
              New Haven, Connecticut   Finance

1969   Temple University   BS
              Philadelphia, Pennsylvania   Marketing

PERSONAL

Age: 42 years   Business Experience: 21 years
Married: 15 years   Years in Management: 19 years
1 son - 10 years old

1. This objective is vague. A Career Summary would highlight the same skills more effectively.

2. All of the experiences are with IBM. Use an overall IBM heading, follow with titles, locations, dates, and experience.

3. This format is choppy and difficult to read.

4. What were the results? Needs expansion.

5. This is repetitive.

6. Stated as $XX million is more effective.

PAMELA AUBREY
18 Oakley Avenue, Pittsburgh, Pennsylvania 15222
(412) 766-9222(b)   (412) 755-4444 (h)

PROFESSIONAL OBJECTIVE

(1) Senior general management position utilizing extensive sales/marketing expertise in a major organization.

PROFESSIONAL EXPERIENCE

REGION MANAGER   1980 – present
(2) IBM Corporation
Pittsburgh, Pennsylvania
(eight branches)
(3) ○ Sales Revenue – $400M annually
○ 2,500 employees (Sales, Service and Administration)
○ #1 NEWS (National Employment Work Survey) Region
○ #1 Service Region
○ #1 Response Time Region
○ Developed an Employee Involvement Program   (4)

REGION MANAGER   1978 – 1980
IBM Corporation
Columbus, Ohio
(six branches)
○ Sales Revenue – $280M annually
○ 1,300 employees
○ #1-in 1979 and 1980

MANAGER, GEM   1976 – 1978
(5) (GOVERNMENT, EDUCATION AND
MEDICAL MARKETING)
IBM Corporation
Stamford, Connecticut
○ 4 employees - staff assignment
○ Responsible for development and implementation of marketing strategies (pricing, advertising, compensation, etc.) for the State, Local, and Federal Government, Education and Medical markets.   (5)

BRANCH MANAGER I   1973 – 1976
IBM Corporation
Hartford, Connecticut
○ Sales Revenue – $40M nationally
○ 290 employees
○ Brought Hartford Branch from 82nd to 1st in Branch Rankings, finishing #2 nationally in Sales and #4 in overall performance. Increased revenues from 27.0 million dollars to approximately
(6) 40.0 million dollars in four years of management
(6)

81

7. How did this individual become the top ranking salesperson?

8. Poor format—tighten this area.

9. Eliminate.

10. This really doesn't add anything to the résumé.

SALES MANAGER   1971 – 1973
IBM Corporation
Hartford, Connecticut
   ○ Six Sales Representatives
(6) ○ Fifteen million dollars in revenue
   ○ #1 Sales Manager in region
   ○ Youngest sales manager in branch history

SALES REPRESENTATIVE   1969 – 1971
IBM Corporation
Hartford, Connecticut
   ○ Managed territory of 1,000 customers
(7) ○ Top ranking sales rep in 1971
   ○ #1 sales rep in New England region in 1970

EDUCATION

| 1973 | Yale University
New Haven, Connecticut | MBA
Finance (8) |
| 1969 | Temple University
Philadelphia, Pennsylvania | BS
Marketing |

PERSONAL

(9) Age: 42 years   Business Experience: 21 years
Married: 15 years   Years in Management: 19 years
1 son – 10 years old   (10)

Comments: The significant accomplishments and career progression need to be highlighted. A career summary would be effective. Accomplishments and skills need to be presented.

PAMELA AUBREY

18 Oakley Avenue
Pittsburgh, Pennsylvania 15222
(412) 766-9222 (B)
(412) 755-4444 (H)

CAREER SUMMARY

20 years of consistent top performance in sales/marketing and a proven record of accomplishment with a Fortune 100 company.

EXPERIENCE

IBM CORPORATION
1969 - present

REGION MANAGER, Pittsburgh, Pennsylvania 1980 - present

Direct staff of 2500 sales, service and administrative employees located in eight branches with an annual sales revenue of $400 million.

- Consistently achieve over 100% of sales targets.
- #1 in Customer Satisfaction Management Survey.
- #1 in National Employment Work Survey (NEWS).
- #1 in Service and Response Time.
- Developed and implemented an Employee Involvement Program, "Excellence Day." Encouraged and motivated employees through interaction with successful role models.
- Made President's Club 7 out of the 10 eligible years.

REGION MANAGER, Columbus, Ohio 1978 - 1980

Directed staff of 1300 sales, service, and administrative employees located in six branches with an annual sales revenue of $280 million.

- Achieved #1 in sales performance in 1979 and 1980.
- Increased service response time by 20%.

MANAGER, GOVERNMENT, EDUCATION, AND MEDICAL MARKETING (GEM), Stamford, Connecticut 1976 - 1978

Developed and implemented marketing strategies (pricing, advertising, and compensation) for State, Local, and Federal markets. Managed staff of four.

BRANCH MANAGER, Hartford, Connecticut 1973 - 1976

Managed staff of 290 employees with annual sales revenue of $40 million.

- Took first place in National Branch Rankings - up from 82nd place.
- #2 Sales branch nationally and #4 in overall performance.
- Increased revenues from $27 million to approximately $40 million.

SALES MANAGER, Hartford, Connecticut 1971 - 1973

Directed staff of six sales representatives, 15 territories, and revenues of $15 million.

- Increased machine population 24%.
- #1 Sales Manager in New England Region.
- Achieved revenue growth of 50%, from $10 million to $15 million.

SALES REPRESENTATIVE, Hartford, Connecticut 1969 - 1971

Managed sales territory of 1000 existing customers. Increased customer base to 5000. Generated $6 million in equipment and supply sales.

- Achieved top ranking national sales representative in 1971.
- #1 sales representative in New England region in 1970.

EDUCATION

Masters in Business Administration, Finance
Yale University, New Haven, Connecticut, 1973

Bachelor of Science in Marketing
Temple University, Philadelphia, Pennsylvania, 1969

DAVID LERNER
45 Tulip Lane
Durham, North Carolina 27708
(919) 667-1555 (H)   (919) 889-3111 (W)

EXPERIENCE

March 1977 - Present   Mobil Oil Company

October 1983 - Present

> Supervisor, Systems Development: Supervising a group of 6
> analysts and programmers; hired personnel; gave performance
> reviews; directed studies and system development projects;
> evaluated proposals from field locations; evaluated new
> products; prepared and negotiated contracts for software and
> services.
>
> Projects included a requirement study for all of the
> distribution and financial systems for a $600 million
> chemical division, an Information Resource Management study
> using the BSP methodology and a system development project for
> an agricultural retail marketing subsidiary.
>
> The programming environment included an IBM AS400 computer,
> IBM PC computers, an IBM S/3090 computer and communications
> between the computers.

February 1978 - October 1983

> Sr. Analyst: Supervised several development projects; systems
> included an inventory and purchasing system for maintenance
> spares, a General Ledger system and an inventory planning
> system; duties included conducting interviews and meetings
> with users; preparing project plans and schedules; writing
> procedure manuals; performing detail design work.
>
> The programming environment included multiple IBM S/36
> computers, CICS with the DL/I interface and communications
> from an IBM S/3081 computer to the IBM S/36 computers.

March 1977 - February 1978

> Systems Analyst: Assisted in the development and implementation of an order
> entry system.

April 1974 - February 1977   Technology Service Corp.

> Member of the Technical Staff: Performed studies under
> contracts for the Environmental Protection Administration;
> developed computer programs for freeway simulations and
> optimization, data analysis and pattern recognition.

November 1972 - February 1974   Miller and Associates

> Systems Analyst: Conducted studies of strategic weapons
> deployments.

EDUCATION

> Duke University, Durham, North Carolina, MS, 1972, Operations
> Research
>
> Drake College of Technology, Atlanta, Georgia, BS, 1970,
> Mechanical Engineering

HONORS

> Membership in Tau Beta Pi and Pi Tau Sigma.

COMMUNITY SERVICE

> President, local Toastmasters club, 1984 - 1985
> Member, Durham Chamber of Commerce, 1979 - 1982

MILITARY SERVICE

> Honorable Discharge from the U.S. Army Reserve, June, 1976.

1. The dates take a prominent position. This needs to be reorganized.

2. Shift in tense. This should all be in the present tense.

3. Too vague. Rewrite to show accomplishments.

4. Hardware and software should be in a separate section.

5. Don't abbreviate.

6. Omit months.

DAVID LERNER
45 Tulip Lane
Durham, North Carolina 27708
(919) 667-1555 (H)   (919) 889-3111 (W)

EXPERIENCE

March 1977 - Present   Mobil Oil Company

(6) October 1983 - Present

Supervisor, Systems Development: Supervising a group of 6 analysts and programmers; hired personnel; gave performance reviews; directed studies and system development projects; evaluated proposals from field locations; evaluated new products; prepared and negotiated contracts for software and services.

(3) Projects included a requirement study for all of the distribution and financial systems for a $600 million chemical division, an Information Resource Management study using the BSP methodology and a system development project for an agricultural retail marketing subsidiary.

(4) The programming environment included an IBM AS400 computer, IBM PC computers, an IBM S/3090 computer and communications between the computers.

February 1978 - October 1983

(5) _Sr. Analyst:_ Supervised several development projects; systems included an inventory and purchasing system for maintenance spares, a General Ledger system and an inventory planning system; duties included conducting interviews and meetings with users; preparing project plans and schedules; writing procedure manuals; performing detail design work.

(4) The programming environment included multiple IBM S/36 computers, CICS with the DL/I interface and communications from an IBM S/3081 computer to the IBM S/36 computers.

March 1977 - February 1978

Systems Analyst: Assisted in the development and implementation of an order entry system.

April 1974 - February 1977   Technology Service Corp.

Member of the Technical Staff: Performed studies under contracts for the Environmental Protection Administration; developed computer programs for freeway simulations and optimization, data analysis and pattern recognition.

7. Omit—include this on the application.

8. Include this only if it has a bearing on the industry you are looking to work in.

RESUME OF DAVID LERNER
Page 2

November 1972 – February 1974   Miller and Associates

Systems Analyst: Conducted studies of strategic weapons deployments.

EDUCATION

Duke University, Durham, North Carolina, MS, 1972, Operations Research

Drake College of Technology, Atlanta, Georgia, BS, 1970, Mechanical Engineering

HONORS

Membership in Tau Beta Pi and Pi Tau Sigma.

(7) COMMUNITY SERVICE

President, local Toastmasters club, 1984 – 1985
Member, Durham Chamber of Commerce, 1979 – 1982

(8) MILITARY SERVICE

Honorable Discharge from the U.S. Army Reserve, June, 1976.

Comments: A résumé for an individual in the computer field must focus on computer experiences. Hardware, software, and areas of study under education should all be highlighted. Organize the résumé so these qualifications are in prominent positions.

DAVID LERNER

45 Tulip Lane, Durham, North Carolina 27708 (919) 667-1555 (H) (919) 889-3111 (W)

Innovative, practical manager with broad experience in SYSTEMS DEVELOPMENT.

EXPERIENCE

Mobil Oil, Durham, North Carolina 1977-present

Supervisor, Systems Development, 1983 - present

Supervise a group of six analysts and programmers; hire, review, and appraise performance. Direct studies and systems development projects, evaluate proposals from field locations, and review new products. Prepare and negotiate contracts for software and services.

Completed a requirement study for all of the distribution and financial systems for a $600 million chemical division; an Information Resource Management study using the BSP methodology; a system development project for an agricultural retail marketing subsidiary.

Senior Analyst, 1978 - 1983

Supervised development projects: an inventory and purchasing system for maintenance spare, a General Ledger system, and an inventory planning system. Conducted interviews and meetings with users, prepared project plans and schedules, wrote procedure manuals, and performed detail design work.

Systems Analyst, 1977 - 1978

Assisted in the development and implementation of an order entry system.

Technology Service Corporation, Atlanta, Georgia, 1974 - 1977

Technical Staff Member

Performed studies for Environmental Protection Agency contracts: developed computer programs for freeway simulations, optimization, data analysis, and pattern recognition.

Miller and Associates, Atlanta, Georgia, 1972 - 1974

Systems Analyst

Conducted studies of strategic weapons deployments.

EDUCATION

MS in Operations Research, Duke University, Durham, North Carolina, 1972
BS in Mechanical Engineering, Drake College of Technology, Atlanta, Georgia, 1970

HONORS Membership in Tau Beta Pi and Pi Tau Sigma

HARDWARE: IBM S/3090, AS/400, S/36, IBM PC-AT

SOFTWARE: IBM MVS/VS, IMS/VS, CICS/VS, CPF, SSP, COBOL, BASIC

SANDRA B. MAGEE

1224 Rollings Road   Fairfax, Virginia 23011

CAREER INTEREST

A position with growth potential in the retailing field.

EDUCATIONAL BACKGROUND

Tobe-Coburn School for Fashion Careers, Certificate of Completion, 1984.

CAREER RELATED COURSEWORK

Retailing; Fashion History; Fabrics; Fashion Promotion; Business
Writing;

Effective Displays; Public Relations; Introduction to Computers.

WORK EXPERIENCE

Hecht Company, Washington, D. C.

Head of Stock, 1984-present

Receive and ticket merchandise and set up displays in the women's
sportswear department. Take inventory, transfer merchandise, and
keep records of department sales. Coordinate all advertising;
mount advertising, set up display and ensure adequate stock of
merchandise.

Bloomingdale's, Tysons Corner, Virginia

Salesclerk, 1983-1984

Arranged merchandise, restocked shelves, and rang up customer sales.
Assisted customers and took inventory. Advised management of special
requests and set up displays.

The Clothes Horse, Fairfax, Virginia

Salesclerk, 1982

Assisted customers in their purchases, arranged displays, unpacked
merchandise and took inventory. Opened and closed the store when
the manager was not available.

Fairfax Toyota, Fairfax, Virginia

Receptionist, 1981

Part-time receptionist. Answered phones and directed calls. Greeted
and directed customers.

REFERENCES FURNISHED UPON REQUEST

90

1. Career interest doesn't sound as committed as Career Objective.

2. This is too vague. What type of position in retailing?

3. Where is the school located? A fashion school in New York City has more prestige than one in Minneapolis.

4. This area can be effective and provide support of various skills and knowledge. It should be longer and can be separate or tied into education.

5. The word ''experience'' by itself is more concise.

6. This can be beefed up. What are the volumes? Both number of pieces and sales revenue. Is this a main store with branches?

7. This area has more responsibility than expressed—expand.

8. Omit the word ''part-time''.

9. If this area can't be expanded, eliminate.

10. Is this necessary? Use the space to present qualifications.

SANDRA B. MAGEE

1224 Rollings Road   Fairfax, Virginia 23011

(1) CAREER INTEREST

A position with growth potential in the retailing field.   (2)

EDUCATIONAL BACKGROUND

(3) Tobe-Coburn School for Fashion Careers, Certificate of Completion, 1984.

(4) CAREER RELATED COURSEWORK

Retailing; Fashion History; Fabrics; Fashion Promotion; Business Writing;

Effective Displays; Public Relations; Introduction to Computers.

(5) WORK EXPERIENCE

Hecht Company, Washington, D. C.

Head of Stock, 1984-present

(6) Receive and ticket merchandise and set up displays in the women's sportswear department. Take inventory, transfer merchandise, and keep records of department sales. Coordinate all advertising; mount advertising, set up display and ensure adequate stock of merchandise.

Bloomingdale's, Tysons Corner, Virginia

Salesclerk, 1983-1984

(7) Arranged merchandise, restocked shelves, and rang up customer sales. Assisted customers and took inventory. Advised management of special requests and set up displays.

The Clothes Horse, Fairfax, Virginia

Salesclerk, 1982

Assisted customers in their purchases, arranged displays, unpacked merchandise and took inventory. Opened and closed the store when the manager was not available.

Fairfax Toyota, Fairfax, Virginia

Receptionist, 1981

(8) Part-time receptionist. Answered phones and directed calls. Greeted (9) and directed customers.

(10)   REFERENCES FURNISHED UPON REQUEST

Comments: Presents candidate as weak on experience and skills. Expand education to support career objective. Develop work experience.

SANDRA B. MAGEE

893-0044

1224 Rollings Road   Fairfax, Virginia 23011

-----CAREER OBJECTIVE--

A position as Assistant Buyer or Department Manager in a fashion
retail operation.

--EDUCATION------------------------------

Tobe-Coburn School for Fashion Careers, New York, New York.
Certificate of Completion, Retailing and Fashion Promotion, 1984.

EDUCATIONAL HIGHLIGHTS

- Assistant Supervisor, Infants at Macy's, Herald Square, New York.
  Spring 1984 work block.

- Salesclerk, Better Dresses at Bloomingdale's, New York, New York.
  Christmas 1983 work block.

- 27 credits in:

Retailing	Business Writing	Introduction to Business
Fashion History	Public Relations	Introduction to Computers
Fabrics	Effective Displays	Fashion Promotion

--EXPERIENCE-----------------------------

Hecht Company, Washington, D.C.   1984 - present
Head of Stock

Coordinate all merchandise for Women's Sportswear department. Receive,
ticket, and transfer merchandise; record, update, and report on department sales. Display merchandise, coordinate advertising and ensure
successful promotions by maintaining proper stock levels.

Bloomingdale's, Tysons Corners, Virginia   1983 - 1984
Salesclerk

Assisted customers, arranged merchandise, restocked shelves and handled
cash and credit sales transactions in the Sportswear department. Communicated special requests and trends to management, took inventory, and
set up displays.

The Clothes Horse, Fairfax, Virginia   1982
Salesclerk

Full range of responsibilities in small retail operation. Opened and
closed store in manager's absence, unpacked and ticketed merchandise,
arranged displays and assisted customers in selection and cash and
credit sales transactions.

CRISTINE E. GORDON
353 Jefferson Avenue
Washington, D. C. 20002
(202) 455-9008 (home)
(202) 970-4289 (office)

Date of Birth: January 20, 1947

EXPERIENCE

Executive Assistant to the Solicitor of Labor, U. S. Department
of Labor, Washington, D. C., October 1982
- present (October 1982 - May 1985, Acting)

     I assist the Solicitor of Labor, who oversees a staff of
approximately 750 people. I review a wide range of
briefs, memoranda and correspondence: provide legal advice
to the Solicitor and other Department of Labor officials on a
variety of issues: perform special tasks and oversee special
projects as assigned by the Solicitor: and act as the
Solicitor's representative on various boards and committees.

Deputy Associate Solicitor, Division of Legislation and Legal
Counsel, U. S. Department of Labor, Washington, D. C., September
1981 - October 1982

     I was responsible for the management of the Division and
for the review of legislative items, legal opinions, labor
relations litigation and litigation under the Freedom of
Information Act. In this capacity, I supervised a staff of
40 people.

Supervisory Attorney, Office of the Solicitor, United States
of Labor, Washington, D. C., July 1978 - September 1981

     As Counsel for Black Lung Benefits, I supervised a staff
of 38 attorneys and 14 support personnel. My primary responsibility was the supervision of appellate litigation before the
federal courts of appeals and the Benefits Review Board of the
Department of Labor and the coordination of trial and appellate
policy.

Trial and Appellate Attorney, Civil Rights Division, United
States Department of Justice, Washington, D. C., July 1972 - June
1978

     From July 1972 to September 1974, I was responsible for the
litigation of cases under the Fair Housing Act of 1968. From
September 1974 through June 1978, I worked in the Appellate
Section, where I was responsible for cases pending in the Supreme
Court and courts of appeals involving school desegregation,
voting rights, equal employment opportunity, housing
discrimination, and the rights of persons in public institutions.

Law Clerk, Pell and Lane, Chicago, Illinois, Summer 1971

     As a summer clerk, I did research and writing, primarily for clients in communications industries.

Writer, National Institute for Education in Law and Poverty, Chicago, Illinois, Summer 1970

     I summarized recent cases and wrote articles for the "Clearinghouse Review," a periodical on public interest law.

Writer, Creative Writing Section, Illinois Bell Telephone Co., Chicago, Illinois, Summer 1969

     I wrote movie scripts, pamphlets, brochures and speeches for the use of company employees.

EDUCATION

Legal: Northwestern University School of Law,
                Chicago, Illinois
                J.D., cum laude, May 1972
                Law Review
                Order of the Coif
                Instructor in legal writing and moot court

College: University of Illinois, Urbana, Illinois
                B.S. in Journalism, summa cum laude, June 1969
                Bronze Tablet award (upper 2% of class)
                Kappa Tau Alpha Journalism award
                Staff Writer, Daily Illini
                Grade point average of 4.8 (on a 5.0 scale)

BAR MEMBERSHIPS

Admitted to the District of Columbia Court of Appeals, January 1973. Member of the bar of the United States Supreme Court and various courts of appeals.

         References and writing samples available upon
         request.

1. Centering the phone numbers throws the heading off. Either center one and place the second number directly below or abbreviate home (h) and office (o) so the numbers are the same length. ①

2. This personal information should ② not be included. The most important information about you should be included right up front.

3. Avoid using pronouns.

4. How do you "assist" and what do you "provide?" Use stronger verbs that convey what you contribute. This work area needs to ③ be developed.

5. What management responsibilities were handled? This is vague and wordy.

6. This is incorrect. It is not United States of Labor, but U.S. Department of Labor.

7. What did the supervision involve? This is too vague.

8. This is inconsistent. In the previous positions, U. S. is abbreviated in the organizational title and here it is spelled out.

CRISTINE E. GORDON
353 Jefferson Avenue
Washington, D. C. 20002
(202) 455-9008 (home)
(202) 970-4289 (office)

Date of Birth: January 20, 1947

EXPERIENCE

Executive Assistant to the Solicitor of Labor, U. S. Department of Labor, Washington, D. C., October 1982 - present (October 1982 - May 1985, Acting) ④

④ I assist the Solicitor of Labor, who oversees a staff of approximately 750 people. I review a wide range of briefs, memoranda and correspondence: provide legal advice to the Solicitor and other Department of Labor officials on a variety of issues: perform special tasks and oversee special projects as assigned by the Solicitor: and act as the Solicitor's representative on various boards and committees.

Deputy Associate Solicitor, Division of Legislation and Legal Counsel, U. S. Department of Labor, Washington, D. C., September 1981 - October 1982

⑤ I was responsible for the management of the Division and for the review of legislative items, legal opinions, labor relations litigation and litigation under the Freedom of Information Act. In this capacity, I supervised a staff of 40 people.

⑥

Supervisory Attorney, Office of the Solicitor, United States of Labor, Washington, D. C., July 1978 - September 1981

⑦

As Counsel for Black Lung Benefits, I supervised a staff of 38 attorneys and 14 support personnel. My primary responsibility was the supervision of appellate litigation before the federal courts of appeals and the Benefits Review Board of the Department of Labor and the coordination of trial and appellate policy.

⑧

Trial and Appellate Attorney, Civil Rights Division, United States Department of Justice, Washington, D. C., July 1972 - June 1978

From July 1972 to September 1974, I was responsible for the litigation of cases under the Fair Housing Act of 1968. From September 1974 through June 1978, I worked in the Appellate Section, where I was responsible for cases pending in the Supreme Court and courts of appeals involving school desegregation, voting rights, equal employment opportunity, housing discrimination, and the rights of persons in public institutions.

9. These experiences should be deleted. The only reason you would include is to show writing skills and experience.

10. Delete the titles "Legal" and "College." The degrees indicate what they are.

11. Writing samples would only be used for an individual applying for a position requiring extensive writing. Delete this and the reference line.

Law Clerk, Pell and Lane, Chicago, Illinois, Summer 1971

    As a summer clerk, I did research and writing, primarily for clients in communications industries.

⑨ Writer, National Institute for Education in Law and Poverty, Chicago, Illinois, Summer 1970

    I summarized recent cases and wrote articles for the "Clearinghouse Review," a periodical on public interest law.

Writer, Creative Writing Section, Illinois Bell Telephone Co., Chicago, Illinois, Summer 1969

    I wrote movie scripts, pamphlets, brochures and speeches for the use of company employees.

EDUCATION

⑩ Legal: Northwestern University School of Law,
               Chicago, Illinois
               J.D., cum laude, May 1972
               Law Review
               Order of the Coif
               Instructor in legal writing and moot court

College: University of Illinois, Urbana, Illinois
               B.S. in Journalism, summa cum laude, June 1969
               Bronze Tablet award (upper 2% of class)
               Kappa Tau Alpha Journalism award
               Staff Writer, Daily Illini
               Grade point average of 4.8 (on a 5.0 scale)

BAR MEMBERSHIPS

Admitted to the District of Columbia Court of Appeals, January 1973. Member of the bar of the United States Supreme Court and various courts of appeals.

⑪   References and writing samples available upon request.

Comments: The format of the résumé does not highlight the individual's strengths. The experience areas all need to be developed.

CRISTINE E. GORDON

353 Jefferson Avenue, Washington, D. C. 20002
(202) 455-9008 (h)
(202) 970-4289 (o)

CAREER SUMMARY: 17 years of experience as a litigator and manager for the Federal Government.

EXPERIENCE

U.S. DEPARTMENT OF LABOR, Washington, D. C.

Executive Assistant to the Solicitor of Labor   1982 - present

Assist the Solicitor in administering a staff of 750. Review a wide range of briefs, memoranda, and correspondence; research prior cases, analyze and summarize documents, and make recommendations for action.

Advise the Solicitor and other Department of Labor officials on a variety of legal issues. Perform special tasks, oversee special projects, and act as the Solicitor's representative on various boards and committees.

Representative for "Tort Reform Working Group", made up of various federal agencies. Formulated a Department of Labor position on "Whistleblower" policy. Representative for "Secretary's Child Care Task Force."

Deputy Associate Solicitor   1981 - 1982

Direct responsibility for Division of Legislation and Legal Counsel and staff of 40; hired, counseled, and evaluated performance.

Prepared budgets; reviewed, edited, made recommendations, and revised legislative items, legal opinions, labor relations litigation, and litigation under the Freedom of Information Act. Implemented a computerized tracking system for cases.

Supervisory Attorney   1978 - 1981

As Counsel for Black Lung Benefits, supervised appellate litigation before the federal courts of appeals and the Benefits Review Board of the Department of Labor and coordinated trial and appellate policy.

Supervised a staff of 38 attorneys and 14 support personnel. Hired staff and conducted training on preparation of appellate briefs and conducting oral arguments for courts of appeals.

UNITED STATES DEPARTMENT OF JUSTICE, Washington, D. C.

Trial and Appellate Attorney   1972 - 1978

> Handled the litigation of cases under the Fair Housing Act of 1968. Prepared briefs in cases pending in the Supreme Court and courts of appeals involving school desegregation, voting rights, equal employment opportunity, housing discrimination, and the rights of persons in public institutions.

EDUCATION

Northwestern University School of Law, Chicago, Illinois
J.D., cum laude, 1972

> Law Review
> Order of the Coif
> Instructor in legal writing and moot court

University of Illinois, Urbana, Illinois
B.S. in Journalism, **summa cum laude,** 1969

> Bronze tablet award (upper 2% of class)
> Kappa Tau Alpha Journalism award
> Staff Writer, <u>Daily Illini</u>
> Grade point average of 4.8 (on a 5.0 scale)

BAR MEMBERSHIPS

Admitted to the District of Columbia Court of Appeals, January 1973. Member of the bar of the United States Supreme Court and various courts of appeals.

PUBLICATIONS

''Recovering Fees from the Government''
  <u>Litigation</u> magazine, Fall 1983

ANTHONY PERILLO

95240 Highland Lane
Rochester, New York 14617
(716) 451-0866 (H)
(716) 455-3422 (O)

EMPLOYMENT

1979 - Present
MONROE COUNTY
Internal Audit Division
15 Bell Highway
Roachester, NY 14602

Auditor III-Current responsibilities include primary supervision of financial, management, and compliance audits of general fund and other County agencies. Responsibilities included in these audits are:

- assigning staff
- preparation of preliminary survey
- preparation of audit program
- performance of fieldwork
- workpaper preparation
- progress briefings with the auditee
- review of all deficiency findings
- review and approval of audit report
- training junior audit staff
- preparation of sampling plan used in test work.

Additional duties include working with the audit director in preparation of the following:

- work with the County Executive and his deputies on special assignments
- long range audit plan
- internal audit manuals
- budget
- annual report to the County Executive
- training of audit staff
- determination of proper utilization of junior audit personnel
- staff performance appraisals
- audits of County licensed bingo operations

Accomplishments in the field of accounting/auditing:

- wrote accounting manual for use by a County agency in dealing with grants (sub grantees)
- assisted in writing a Bingo Accounting Guide
- currently studying to finish passing the Certified Internal Auditor Exam

- have taken courses in basic EDP and COBOL
- attended seminars in contract fraud, operational audits, fraud audits, EDP auditing, report writing, internal control review, communicating audit findings, use of statistical sampling in auditing.

1978 - 1979 PAUL G. TRAP, LTD. PO Box 5477 Rochester, NY	Senior Staff Auditor. Responsibilities included Auditor-in-Charge of CETA, Federal Credit Unions, and HUD audits. Training of other staff personnel for audit of government grants. Monthly client write-up and review. Consultation with clients (primarily non-profit) on effective accounting systems, budgetary procedures, and preparation of manuals. In addition, supervision and preparation of management and compliance audits were a major part of the position.
1977 - 1978 SELF-EMPLOYED	Responsible to clients which were non-profit, retail, service, and individual tax returns. Experience includes audits for Department of Labor (CETA), Housing and Urban Development, and Federal Credit Unions in the areas of internal audit, budget preparation, computerized books, and all other accounting/auditing functions.
1975 - 1977 ASSOCIATES FOR BETTER ROADS 1199 St. Paul Blvd. Rochester, NY	Employed as Comptroller and Office Manager. Responsibilities included contracts and funds received for federal and private foundation grants, direct and indirect costs, and all other phases of accounting operations.

EDUCTION

1970 - 1974	Rochester Institute of Technology
	Rochester, NY
	  Degree: DCS
	  Major: Accounting

1. Use active verbs.

2. These are all tasks in the audit function and read like a job description.

3. Omit until you have passed the entire exam—then include under certification.

4. Use a separate section to indicate professional training.

5. Accomplishments are hidden.

6. Too much white space.

7. Omit address. It leaves you open to prospective employers randomly calling previous employers for references.

ANTHONY PERILLO

95240 Highland Lane
Rochester, New York 14617
(716) 451-0866 (H)
(716) 455-3422 (O)

EMPLOYMENT

Auditor III-Current responsibilities include primary supervision of financial, management, and compliance audits of general fund and other County agencies. Responsibilities included in these audits are:

- assigning staff
- preparation of preliminary survey
- preparation of audit program
- performance of fieldwork
- workpaper preparation
- progress briefings with the auditee
- review of all deficiency findings
- review and approval of audit report
- training junior audit staff
- preparation of sampling plan used in test work.

Additional duties include working with the audit director in preparation of the following:

- work with the County Executive and his deputies on special assignments
- long range audit plan
- internal audit manuals
- budget
- annual report to the County Executive
- training of audit staff
- determination of proper utilization of junior audit personnel
- staff performance appraisals
- audits of County licensed bingo operations

Accomplishments in the field of accounting/auditing:

- wrote accounting manual for use by a County agency in dealing with grants (sub grantees)
- assisted in writing a Bingo Accounting Guide
- currently studying to finish passing the Certified Internal Auditor Exam

- have taken courses in basic EDP and COBOL
- attended seminars in contract fraud, operational audits, fraud audits, EDP auditing, report writing, internal control review, communicating audit findings, use of statistical sampling in auditing.

1979 - Present
MONROE COUNTY
Internal Audit Division
15 Bell Highway
Roachester, NY 14602

8. "Responsibilities" is redundant and in the passive voice. Choose active verbs.

9. Weak—use: "supervised and prepared management and compliance audits."

10. Typo. Should be "BCS".

11. Indicate only the year degree was received.

12. Accounting Consultant sounds more professional.

13. Misspelled word.

1978 - 1979
PAUL G. TRAP, LTD.
PO Box 5477
Rochester, NY

 Senior Staff Auditor. Responsibilities included Auditor-in-Charge of CETA, Federal Credit Unions, and HUD audits. Training of other staff personnel for audit of government grants. Monthly client write-up and review. Consultation with clients (primarily non-profit) on effective accounting systems, budgetary procedures, and preparation of manuals. In addition, supervision and preparation of management and compliance audits were a major part of the position.

⑨

⑫ 1977 - 1978
SELF-EMPLOYED

Responsible to clients which were non-profit, retail, service, and individual tax returns. Experience includes audits for Department of Labor (CETA), Housing and Urban Development, and Federal Credit Unions in the areas of internal audit, budget preparation, computerized books, and all other accounting/auditing functions.

1975 - 1977
ASSOCIATES FOR BETTER ROADS
1199 St. Paul Blvd.
Rochester, NY

Employed as Comptroller and Office Manager. Responsibilities included contracts and funds received for federal and private foundation grants, direct and indirect costs, and all other phases of accounting operations.

 EDUCTION

⑪ 1970 - 1974

Rochester Institute of Technology
Rochester, NY
 Degree: DCS ⑩
 Major: Accounting

Comments: This résumé is out of balance. The paragraphs are too narrow and too heavy. It has poor eye appeal and is difficult to read. The résumé reads like a job description. There are accomplishments but they are hidden. This résumé could easily fit on one page and effectively emphasize accounting credentials.

ANTHONY PERILLO

95240 Highland Lane, Rochester, New York 14617 (h)716/451-0866 (o) 716/455-3422

OBJECTIVE   An audit management position in private industry.

EXPERIENCE

1979
to
present

Audit Supervisor, Monroe County, Rochester, New York

Supervise and conduct financial management and compliance audits of county agencies for a large local government with annual budget in excess of one billion dollars. Conduct special assignments for senior county management. Wrote an accounting manual used by grant recipients. Co-authored an accounting guide for nonprofit organizations conducting bingo games and raffles.

1978–1979   **Senior Staff Auditor,** Paul G. Trap, Ltd., Rochester, New York.

Prepared and supervised federal compliance audits for Comprehensive Employ- ment Training Act (CETA), Federal Credit Unions, and Housing and Urban Development (HUD) grants. Trained staff to comply with grant requirements. Provided management advisory services to clients in accounting systems design, required budget practices, and procedures manuals.

1977–1978   **Accounting Consultant,** Rochester, New York.

Provided accounting services to clients on a consulting basis. Client base con- sisted of nonprofit organizations, retail, and service industry. Assisted in the areas of internal audit, budget preparation, and conversion to computerized systems. Prepared individual tax returns.

1975–1977   **Comptroller,** Associates for Better Roads, Rochester, New York.

Handled contracts and funds for federal and private foundation grants, direct and indirect costs, and all additional accounting operations.

EDUCATION

Bachelor of Commercial Sciences in Accounting, 1974.
Rochester Institute of Technology, Rochester, New York.

PROFESSIONAL
  TRAINING

Seminars by the Institute of Internal Auditors: Contract Fraud, Operational Audits, Fraud Audits, EDP Auditing, Report Writing, Internal Control Review, Statistical Sampling, and Communicating Audit Findings.

ASSOCIATIONS

Association of Governmental Accountants
Institute of Internal Auditors

NAME: Gerald Kline

HOME ADDRESS: 2443 K Street, NW
                       Washington, D. C. 20045
                       (202) 432-9665

EDUCATION: Currently working on a Doctoral Degree in
                       Public Administration through NOVA University,
                       Ft. Lauderdale, Florida

                       B.A. (International Relations), from the
                       niversity of South Florida, Tampa, FL – 1971

PROFESSIONAL   Certified Association Executive (C.A.E.) from
  CERTIFICATION: he American Society of Association
                       xecutives, Washington, D.C., 1981

MILITARY SERVICE: U.S. Marine Corps Reserve (1967-1973)
                       NCOIC of Air Intelligence Section-VMA-142

CURRENT POSITION: Executive Director
                       International Association of Fire Chiefs (IAFC)
                       1985-present

                 Ultimate staff authority and accountability for
                 headquarters and IAFC activities: manage and
                 ort the achievement of all programs, establish
                 measurable goals and objectives for financial
                 bility and growth, organizational stability and
                 professional staff development, membership retention
                 and growth, membership services and liaison with
                 manage expenditures and revenues, approve and support
                 administrative policies.

PAST POSITION: Executive Director
                       Florida Chapter, American College of Emergency Physicians
                       1974-1985

                 Directly responsible for the day-to-day operation of
                 a professional physicians association with over 500
                 members; responsible for all program development
                 including both professional and management continuing
                 education conferences; introduced MBO planning
                 procedures for the long-range guidance of the
                 association's activities; responsible for the
                 development and administration of the association's
                 annual budget (about $250,000); identify a need for,
                 plan, develop and organize conferences.

PAST CONCURRENT: Battalion Chief-Reserve
                        Orange County Fire Department, 1982-1985

                 Responsible for the development and implementation
                 of an innovative reserve firefighter program in a

104

county-wide fire department. The program consists of
125 reserve personnel, combat and noncombat
status.

PREVIOUS
  POSITION HELD:

Chairman and Member
Board of Fire Commissioners, Killarney Fire
Control District, (1978-1981)

Responsible for the overall supervision of the operation of the
fire department with 25 paid
and 30 volunteer firefighting and support personnel;
responsible for the development and supervision of
the department's annual budget (about $850,000);
accomplishments as Commissioner included: implemented
affirmative action plan, implemented computer aided
dispatch system, and increased staff size.

PAST
  EMPLOYMENT:

Manager, Convention Services Division
American College of Emergency Physicians
Lansing, Michigan (1973-1974)

Responsible for the planning and operation of two
national conferences.

Emergency Medical Services Specialist
American College of Emergency Physicians
Lansing, Michigan (1973-1974)

Resource person for the national headquarters for all
aspects of emergency medical services.

Consultant
Florida Division of Health
Tallahassee, Florida (1972-1973)

Responsible for development, planning, implementation
of pre-hospital emergency medical services.

FACULTY
  APPOINTMENT:

Adjunct Faculty Member (Executive Development
Program, National Fire Academy, US Fire
Administration, Washington, D.C., 1980-current

ADVISORY
  APPOINTMENTS:

Member, Editorial Resource Panel
EMS Management Advisor
Aspen Systems Corporation, 1984-1988

Member, Advisory Board
JEMS Magazine, 1982-present

MEMBERSHIPS:

American Society of Association Executives
International Association of Fire Chiefs
Resarch Committee on Disasters

MAJOR PUBLICATIONS:	<u>Your First Response in the Streets</u> Co-author; Little, Brown & Company, Boston, Massachusetts (published summer 1984) <u>Developing Communications Programs for Fire Service Agencies</u> United States Fire Administration, National Fire Academy, Washington, D. C., 1980 <u>Emergency Medical Services Implementation Manual</u> Michigan Association of Regional Medical Programs: Lansing, Michigan, 1974
PRESENTATIONS GIVEN:	"Understanding What Happens in Disaster Operations" 1989 International Disaster Management Conference, Orlando, FL, February 1989 Master of Ceremonies, "Ninth Annual Virginia EMS Symposium" Tysons Corner, VA, October 1988 "The Future of Fire Service Training: Where Do We Go From Here?" Maine Fire Chiefs Association, Portland, ME, October 1988 "Incident Command and Operations at Bus Accident Scenes" 54th Annual Convention, Virginia Association of Volunteer Rescue Squads, Virginia Beach, VA, September 1988
ARTICLES PUBLISHED:	"The IAFC Goes Truly International" <u>Fire International</u> (Published in the UK) December 1986/January 1987 "Zero-Based EMS Training" <u>Fire Chief</u>, November 1986 "An Overview of the Private Sector Fire Service" <u>International Fire Chief</u>, February 1984 "Shifting Gears from Fire to EMS Operations" <u>Fire Engineering</u>, November 1983

1. Omit these headings.

2. Too many headings. Include all the positions under "Experience." The dates will indicate what is present, past, and concurrent.

3. Use a consistent format for both education entries.

4. This sounds like a job description. What has been accomplished?

5. "Responsible" is redundant. Choose verbs in the active voice.

6. Fire fighter is spelled incorrectly.

NAME: ① Gerald Kline

HOME ADDRESS: 2443 K Street, NW
Washington, D. C. 20045
(202) 432-9665

EDUCATION: Currently working on a Doctoral Degree in
Public Administration through NOVA University,
③ Ft. Lauderdale, Florida

B.A. (International Relations), from the
niversity of South Florida, Tampa, FL – 1971

PROFESSIONAL
CERTIFICATION: Certified Association Executive (C.A.E.) from
he American Society of Association
xecutives, Washington, D.C., 1981

MILITARY SERVICE: U.S. Marine Corps Reserve (1967-1973)
NCOIC of Air Intelligence Section-VMA-142

CURRENT POSITION: Executive Director
② International Association of Fire Chiefs (IAFC)
1985-present

④ Ultimate staff authority and accountability for
headquarters and IAFC activities: manage and
ort the achievement of all programs, establish
measurable goals and objectives for financial
bility and growth, organizational stability and
professional staff development, membership retention
and growth, membership services and liaison with
manage expenditures and revenues, approve and support
administrative policies.

PAST POSITION: Executive Director
Florida Chapter, American College of Emergency Physicians
1974-1985

⑤ Directly responsible for the day-to-day operation of
a professional physicians association with over 500
members; responsible for all program development
including both professional and management continuing
education conferences; introduced MBO planning
procedures for the long-range guidance of the
association's activities; responsible for the
development and administration of the association's
annual budget (about $250,000); identify a need for,
plan, develop and organize conferences.

PAST CONCURRENT: Battalion Chief-Reserve
⑤ Orange County Fire Department, 1982-1985

⑥ Responsible for the development and implementation
of an innovative reserve firefighter program in a

7. The second parenthesis is missing.

county-wide fire department. The program consists of 125 reserve personnel, combat and noncombat status.

PREVIOUS
POSITION HELD:
Chairman and Member
Board of Fire Commissioners, Killarney Fire
Control District, (1978-1981)

(5) Responsible for the overall supervision of the operation of the fire department with 25 paid and 30 volunteer firefighting and support personnel; responsible for the development and supervision of the department's annual budget (about $850,000); accomplishments as Commissioner included: implemented affirmative action plan, implemented computer aided dispatch system, and increased staff size.

PAST
EMPLOYMENT:
Manager, Convention Services Division
American College of Emergency Physicians
Lansing, Michigan (1973-1974)

(5) Responsible for the planning and operation of two national conferences.

Emergency Medical Services Specialist
American College of Emergency Physicians
Lansing, Michigan (1973-1974)

Resource person for the national headquarters for all aspects of emergency medical services.

Consultant
Florida Division of Health
Tallahassee, Florida (1972-1973)

(5) Responsible for development, planning, implementation of pre-hospital emergency medical services.

FACULTY
APPOINTMENT:
(7) Adjunct Faculty Member (Executive Development Program, National Fire Academy, US Fire Administration, Washington, D.C., 1980-current

ADVISORY
APPOINTMENTS:
Member, Editorial Resource Panel
EMS Management Advisor
Aspen Systems Corporation, 1984-1988

Member, Advisory Board
JEMS Magazine, 1982-present

MEMBERSHIPS:
American Society of Association Executives
International Association of Fire Chiefs
Resarch Committee on Disasters

8. Be consistent in format. Omit parentheses.

9. Don't abbreviate.

MAJOR
PUBLICATIONS:

<u>Your First Response in the Streets</u>
   Co-author; Little, Brown & Company, Boston,
   Massachusetts (published summer 1984) **(8)**

<u>Developing Communications Programs for Fire
Service Agencies</u>
   United States Fire Administration, National
   Fire Academy, Washington, D. C., 1980

<u>Emergency Medical Services Implementation
Manual</u>
   Michigan Association of Regional Medical
   Programs: Lansing, Michigan, 1974

PRESENTATIONS
   GIVEN:

''Understanding What Happens in Disaster
Operations''
   1989 International Disaster Management
   Conference, Orlando, FL, February 1989 **(9)**

Master of Ceremonies, ''Ninth Annual Virginia
EMS Symposium''
   Tysons Corner, VA, October 1988

''The Future of Fire Service Training: Where Do
We Go From Here?''
   Maine Fire Chiefs Association, Portland, ME,
   October 1988

''Incident Command and Operations at Bus
Accident Scenes''
   54th Annual Convention, Virginia Association
   of Volunteer Rescue Squads, Virginia Beach,
   VA, September 1988

ARTICLES
   PUBLISHED:

''The IAFC Goes Truly International''
   <u>Fire International</u> (Published in the UK) **(9)**
   December 1986/January 1987

''Zero-Based EMS Training''
   <u>Fire Chief</u>, November 1986

''An Overview of the Private Sector Fire
Service''
   <u>International Fire Chief</u>, February 1984

''Shifting Gears from Fire to EMS Operations''
   <u>Fire Engineering</u>, November 1983

Comments: Too many headings make this difficult to read. The credentials are important and the résumé (or curriculum vitae) needs to be organized and presented in a format that is easy to follow.

CURRICULUM VITAE

GERALD KLINE, C. A. E.
2443 K Street, NW, Washington, D. C. 20045
(202) 433-0900 (w) (202) 432-9665 (h)

EXPERIENCE

International Association of Fire Chiefs (IAFC), Washington, D.C.
EXECUTIVE DIRECTOR 1985 - present

Direct responsibility to implement and manage programs and services of 10,000 member professional association for senior fire and emergency service managers with an annual budget of $2.2 million.

- Repositioned organization as the leading spokesman for national fire service.
- Net membership increased by 20%; from 6,568 to 7,733.
- Operating revenues increased from $1.3 to $2.2 million.

Manage a staff of 20; 15 professionals and 5 clericals; recruit, interview, hire, and fire; create standards of performance, review performance; counsel employees, train and provide training services.

American College of Emergency Physicians, Florida Chapter, Orlando, Florida
EXECUTIVE DIRECTOR 1974 - 1985

Managed the day-to-day operation of a professional physician's association with over 500 members. Developed and administered an annual budget of approximately $250,000. Planned and implemented program development for professional and management continuing education conferences; planned, developed, and organized ten major and ten smaller multi-agency educational conferences.

Orange County Fire Department (OCFD), Orlando, Florida
BATTALION CHIEF - RESERVE, 1982 - 1985

Developed and implemented an innovative reserve fire fighter program in a county-wide fire department. Program consisted of 125 reserve personnel (combat and noncombat status) with over 85% of the combat personnel maintaining complete Florida State minimum fire fighting certification and 50% having EMT certification.

- Implemented a county-wide reserve-staffed flying manpower squad for peak alarm period. The program contributed over 30,000 man-hours per year to the OCFD, or approximately $50,000.

110

Board of Fire Commissioners, Killarney Fire Control District, Orlando, Florida

    CHAIRMAN AND MEMBER 1978 - 1981

Direct responsibility for overall supervision and operation of fire department with 25 paid and 30 volunteer fire fighting and support personnel. Developed and supervised department's annual budget of $850,000.

- Implemented a pre-hospital advanced life support paramedic program, affirmative action plan, and computer aided dispatch system.

American College of Emergency Physicians, Lansing, Michigan

    MANAGER, CONVENTION SERVICES DIVISION 1973 - 1974

Planned two national conferences with program budgets in excess of $500,000.

    EMERGENCY MEDICAL SERVICES SPECIALIST 1973 - 1974

Resource person for the national headquarters for all aspects of emergency medical services.

MILITARY SERVICE

U. S. Marine Corps Reserve - 1967 - 1973
NCOIC of Air Intelligence Section - VMA - 142

FACULTY APPOINTMENT

Adjunct Faculty Member - Executive Development Program
National Fire Academy, United States Fire Administration
Washington, D. C. 1980 - present

ADVISORY APPOINTMENTS

Member, Advisory Board
JEMS Magazine, 1982 - present

Member, Editorial Resource Panel
EMS Management Advisor
Aspen Systems Corporation, 1984 - 1988

Member, Editorial Advisory Panel
Emergency Medical Service Magazine, 1983 - 1987

EDUCATION

Completed major coursework towards **Doctoral** degree in Public Administration, NOVA University, Ft. Lauderdale, Florida

Bachelor of Arts in International Relations, University of South Florida, Tampa, Florida, 1971

111

PROFESSIONAL CERTIFICATION

Certified Association Executive (C.A.E.) from the American
Society of Association Executives, Washington, D. C., 1981

MEMBERSHIPS

International Association of Fire Chiefs
International Society of Fire Service Instructors
Research Committee on Disasters
American Society of Association Executives

MAJOR PUBLICATIONS

Your First Response In The Streets
   Co-author; Little, Brown & Company, Boston, Massachusetts, 1984

Developing Communications Programs For Fire Service Agencies
   United States Fire Administration, National Fire Academy,
   Washington, D. C., 1980

Emergency Medical Services Implementation Manual
   Michigan Association of Regional Medical Programs, Lansing,
   Michigan, 1974

PRESENTATIONS

"Understanding What Happens In Disaster Operations"
   1989 International Disaster Management Conference, Orlando,
   Florida, February 1989

Master of Ceremonies, "Ninth Annual Virginia EMS Symposium"
   Tysons Corner, Virginia, October 1988

"The Future of Fire Service Training: Where Do We Go From Here?"
   Maine Fire Chiefs Association, Portland, Maine, October 1988

PUBLISHED ARTICLES

"The IAFC Goes Truly International"
   Fire International (Published in the United Kingdom),
   December 1986/January 1987

"Zero-Based EMS Training"
   Fire Chief, November 1986

"An Overview of the Private Sector Fire Service"
   International Fire Chief, February 1984

EMILY DEINER

1700 Butterfield Road
Cleveland, Ohio 47200
(216) 777-1000 (w) (216) 778-3255 (h)

SUMMARY

Nineteen years of progressively responsible experience in Vocational Education, Adult Education, and Community Education in Cuyahoga County Public Schools. Responsible for providing leadership in the development and implementation of adult and community education that are exemplary in the nation.

EXPERIENCE

Director of Adult and Community Education – 1980 to present.
Provides leadership in a program enrolling more than 48,000 students per year.

Director of Vocational and Adult Services – 1975 to 1980.
Provided leadership for the continuing operation of a Vocational Education Program in which more than 37,000 high school students and 18,000 adults are enrolled.

Director of Instruction – 1974-1975. Responsible for implementation of Program of Studies curriculum development system.

Coordinator of Adult Education – 1969-1974. Developed program for Cuyahoga County Public Schools

Teacher – social studies – Cuyahoga County 1966-1968.

EDUCATION

M.Ed. –Bowling Green University, 1967
B.A. –Kent State University, 1965

RECOGNITIONS

–Named the Outstanding Adult Educator for the State of Ohio by the Ohio Association of Public Continuing Adult Education, 1972.

–Awarded a Certificate of Recognition for Outstanding Legislative Achievements on Behalf of Adult Education. Directed a lobbying effort that resulted in a 300% increase in the state appropriation for adult education 1977.

–Named the "Outstanding Citizen of the Year" for the State of Ohio for 1979 by the Ohio Chapter of the National Association of Social Workers.

–Received the Cuyahoga County Human Rights Commission Award for 1982.

–Held public office as a member of the Ohio House of Delegates, 1978-80, 1982-present.

1. The word "education" is redundant.

2. This is grammatically incorrect. Needs to be rephrased.

3. How or to whom is leadership provided?

4. This should be in the past tense.

5. The major accomplishments just don't come through. Summary and experience should be strengthened.

6. "Honors" would be a better heading for this.

7. Reverse order—begin with the most current and work backwards.

8. Indicate location of schools.

EMILY DEINER

1700 Butterfield Road
Cleveland, Ohio 47200
(216) 777-1000 (w) (216) 778-3255 (h)

SUMMARY

Nineteen years of progressively responsible experience in Vocational Education, Adult Education, and Community Education in Cuyahoga County Public Schools. Responsible for providing leadership in the development and implementation of adult and community education that are exemplary in the nation.

EXPERIENCE

Director of Adult and Community Education – 1980 to present.
    Provides leadership in a program enrolling more than 48,000 students per year.
Director of Vocational and Adult Services – 1975 to 1980.
    Provided leadership for the continuing operation of a Vocational Education Program in which more than 37,000 high school students and 18,000 adults are enrolled.
Director of Instruction – 1974-1975. Responsible for implementation of Program of Studies curriculum development system.
Coordinator of Adult Education – 1969-1974. Developed program for Cuyahoga County Public Schools
Teacher – social studies – Cuyahoga County 1966-1968.

EDUCATION

M.Ed. –Bowling Green University, 1967
B.A. –Kent State University, 1965

RECOGNITIONS

–Named the Outstanding Adult Educator for the State of Ohio by the Ohio Association of Public Continuing Adult Education, 1972.

–Awarded a Certificate of Recognition for Outstanding Legislative Achievements on Behalf of Adult Education. Directed a lobbying effort that resulted in a 300% increase in the state appropriation for adult education 1977.

–Named the "Outstanding Citizen of the Year" for the State of Ohio for 1979 by the Ohio Chapter of the National Association of Social Workers.

–Received the Cuyahoga County Human Rights Commission Award for 1982.

–Held public office as a member of the Ohio House of Delegates, 1978-80, 1982-present.

Comments: This résumé is weak. It needs the experience area beefed up and a format that shows the contributions made to the organization.

EMILY DEINER
1700 Butterfield Road, Cleveland, Ohio 47200
(216) 777-1000 (W) (216) 778-3255 (H)

Nineteen years of progressively responsible positions in vocational, adult, and community education. Led an adult education program from start-up to one of the largest and most successful in the United States.

EXPERIENCE

CUYAHOGA COUNTY PUBLIC SCHOOLS, 1966 - present

Director of Adult and Community Education 1980 - present

Provide leadership to a staff of 40 coordinating an adult and community education program serving 4800 students per year. Developed and implemented business, home economics, English As A Second Language (ESL), and External Diploma programs.

Director of Vocational and Adult Services 1975 - 1980

Established a vocational education program that met the needs of 37,000 high school students and 18,000 adults. Designed the program; hired staff.

Director of Instruction 1974 - 1975

Initiated a Program of Studies curriculum development system.

Coordinator of Adult Education 1969 - 1974

Created and implemented the initial Adult Education program for Cuyahoga county.

Teacher, Social Studies 1966 - 1968

EDUCATION

M.Ed. Bowling Green University, Bowling Green, Ohio, 1967
B.A. Kent State University, Kent, Ohio, 1965

HONORS

Member of the Ohio House of Delegates, 1978-1980, 1982-present

Received the Cuyahoga County Human Rights Commission Award, 1982

Named the "Outstanding Citizen of the Year" for the State of Ohio, 1979, by the Ohio Chapter of the National Association of Social Workers

Awarded a Certificate of Recognition for Outstanding Legislative Achievements on Behalf of Adult Education. Directed a lobbying effort that resulted in a 300% increase in the state appropriation for adult education, 1977

Named the Outstanding Adult Educator for the State of Ohio by the Ohio Association of Public Continuing Adult Education, 1972

YOLANDA WILLIAMS

26 Congress Street
Jackson, Mississippi 55006
(226) 889-1142

EMPLOYMENT

Peterson and Lane, Inc.
Jackson, Mississippi

Vice-President	Elected May 1985
Senior Account Executive	November 1984 to Present
Assistant Vice-President	Elected May 1983
Account Executive	January 1982 to November 1984

Senior Account Executive responsible for coverage design,
marketing and negotiating with underwriters, interfacing
with clients to maintain, administer and coordinate international risk management programs and integrate with
domestic coverage placements.

Current clients represent full spectrum of American Multinational Fortune 500 and 1000 Companies: professional
services, design construction, engineering, chemical and
food industries.

Personally responsible for international premium volume
of 6.4 million dollars

International Life Underwriters, Jackson, Mississippi

Casualty Manager	January 1979 to January 1982
Senior Underwriter	June 1977 to January 1979

Responsible for managing, budgeting, personnel, planning,
and coordinating casualty underwriting department. Created
branch office underwriter training program. Participated
in International Life Underwriters Executive "Fast Track"
program.

International Life Underwriters
New York, New York

Junior Underwriter	January 1977 to June 1977
Casualty Underwriter Trainee	June 1975 to January 1977

Assisted underwriters in the review, evaluation selection,
acceptance, pricing and servicing of casualty accounts.
Became familiar with foreign insurance regulations. Developed knowledge and experience in rating procedures/manual
ussage and underwriting skills. Participated in the International Life Underwriters Career Training Program.

116

EDUCATION

NEW YORK UNIVERSITY - B. S. Languages, 1975

School of Languages and Linguistics
Dean's List
Cumulative Average: 3.42
Area of Concentration: Spanish

UNIVERSITY OF MADRID, Spain - Junior Year Abroad Program, 1973-74

Cultural Exchange visit to Mexico - Summer, 1972

CAREER RELATED EDUCATION

Insurance Principles and Practices, sponsored by International
Life Underwriters Education Department, accredited by the College
of Insurance, New York.

Counselor Selling, Wilson Learning Corporation.

Effective Business Writers, College of Insurance, New York.

Fundamentals of Finance and Accounting for the Non-Financial
Executive, The Wharton School of the University of Pennsylvania.

1. Inconsistent. Either have the city and state all on one line or under the organization.

2. Omit months.

3. Use active verbs.

4. Omit months.

5. Expand managed and personnel.

6. Inconsistent. Why is one training program in quotes and the other isn't?

YOLANDA WILLIAMS

26 Congress Street
Jackson, Mississippi 55006
(226) 889-1142

EMPLOYMENT

(1) Peterson and Lane, Inc.
Jackson, Mississippi

Vice-President	Elected May 1985
Senior Account Executive	November 1984 to Present (2)
Assistant Vice-President	Elected May 1983
Account Executive (3)	January 1982 to November 1984

Senior Account Executive responsible for coverage design, marketing and negotiating with underwriters, interfacing with clients to maintain, administer and coordinate international risk management programs and integrate with domestic coverage placements.

Current clients represent full spectrum of American Multinational Fortune 500 and 1000 Companies: professional services, design construction, engineering, chemical and food industries.

Personally responsible for international premium volume of 6.4 million dollars

(1) International Life Underwriters, Jackson, Mississippi

Casualty Manager	January 1979 to January 1982 (4)
Senior Underwriter (5)	June 1977 to January 1979

(3) Responsible for managing, budgeting, personnel, planning, and coordinating casualty underwriting department. Created branch office underwriter training program. Participated in International Life Underwriters Executive "Fast Track" program.

International Life Underwriters (6)
New York, New York

Junior Underwriter	January 1977 to June 1977
Casualty Underwriter Trainee	June 1975 to January 1977

(3) Assisted underwriters in the review, evaluation selection, acceptance, pricing and servicing of casualty accounts. Became familiar with foreign insurance regulations. Developed knowledge and experience in rating procedures/manual ussage and underwriting skills. Participated in the International Life Underwriters Career Training Program. (6)

118

7. Omit.

8. Spell out degree. Don't abbreviate.

9. Include city and state.

10. Format these the same as the above education.

11. There needs to be consistency. Include the city and state where training occurred.

12. Too much white space.

---

⑦ YOLANDA WILLIAMS

EDUCATION   ⑧

    NEW YORK UNIVERSITY - B. S. Languages, 1975

        School of Languages and Linguistics
        Dean's List
        Cumulative Average: 3.42
        Area of Concentration: Spanish

    UNIVERSITY OF MADRID, Spain - Junior Year Abroad Program, 1973-74

    Cultural Exchange visit to Mexico - Summer, 1972

CAREER RELATED EDUCATION

    Insurance Principles and Practices, sponsored by International
    Life Underwriters Education Department, accredited by the College
    of Insurance, New York.

⑪   Counselor Selling, Wilson Learning Corporation.

    Effective Business Writers, College of Insurance, New York.

    Fundamentals of Finance and Accounting for the Non-Financial
    Executive, The Wharton School of the University of Pennsylvania.

⑫

Comments: Needs a career objective or summary to tie this together. Lacks consistency in format. Verbs in the passive voice are weak and don't support the skills and experience needed for upward mobility.

YOLANDA WILLIAMS
26 Congress Street
Jackson, Mississippi 55006
(226) 889-1142 (H)
(226) 887-3297 (B)

CAREER HIGHLIGHTS

11 years of casualty and risk management experience.

- Design coverage to meet an industry's unique needs.

- Manage a client base of Fortune 500 - 1000 companies.

- Experience with foreign insurance regulations.

EXPERIENCE

Peterson and Lane, Inc., Jackson, Mississippi.

Vice-President	Elected 1985
Senior Account Executive	1984-Present
Assistant Vice-President	Elected 1983
Account Executive	1982-1984

Design coverage, market, and negotiate with underwriters.
Maintain, administer, and coordinate international risk management
programs and integrate with domestic coverage placements.

Current clients represent full spectrum of American multinational
Fortune 500 and 1000 Companies: professional services, design
construction, engineering, chemical, and food industries.

Personally responsible for international premium volume of 6.4
million dollars.

International Life Underwriters, Jackson, Mississippi.

Casualty Manager	1979-1982
Senior Underwriter	1977-1979

Opened and managed branch casualty underwriting department. Hired
exempt personnel, developed standards of performance, supervised,
appraised performance, counseled, and dismissed staff. Planned
annual budget of 3 million dollars.

Brought in 20 new accounts. Developed department from one to four
person staff. Created branch underwriter training program.
Participated in International Life Underwriters Executive Fast
Track program.

International Life Underwriters, New York, New York.

Junior Underwriter	1977
Casualty Underwriter Trainee	1975-1977

Reviewed, evaluated, selected, accepted, priced, and serviced casualty accounts while assisting underwriters. Gained understanding of foreign insurance regulations. Developed knowledge and experience in rating procedures/manual usage and underwriting skills. Participated in the International Life Underwriters Career Training Program.

EDUCATION

New York University, New York, New York
Bachelor of Science, Languages, 1975
Area of Concentration: Spanish
Dean's List

University of Madrid, Madrid, Spain
Junior Year Abroad Program, 1973–74

Cultural Exchange Visit, Mexico
Summer, 1972

PROFESSIONAL TRAINING

Insurance Principles and Practices, International Life Underwriters, accredited by the College of Insurance, New York, New York.

Counselor Selling, Wilson Learning Corporation, New York, New York.

Effective Business Writers, College of Insurance, New York, New York.

Fundamentals of Finance and Accounting for the Non-Financial Executive, the Wharton School of the University of Pennsylvania, Philadelphia, Pennsylvania.

LICENSES

Mississippi Brokers License

ASSOCIATIONS

American Association of Casualty Underwriters
Casualty Underwriters Training Council

Charles N. Taylor, CPPO
75 Cedar Drive
Charleston, West Virginia 25305
304-788-3200 (H), 304-908-5500 (W)

Education:

B.S. West Virginia University
M.S. Logistics Management, Air Force Institute of Technology

Work History:

1980-Present:

Director, Purchasing and Supply Management Agency, Charleston
County, West Virginia. Responsible for central purchasing for
county government and school system, and supply management
system for county governmental activities. Direct major agency
of over 50 personnel with annual purchasing volume in excess
of $100 million. Responsible for development and
implementation of integrated purchasing and inventory
management automated system.

1979-1980:

Senior Buyer, West Virginia University, and Purchasing Manager
for the University Medical Center. Responsible for planning,
budgeting, and purchasing medical supplies, equipment, and
services to support major medical center. Supervised a staff
of two professional buyers and an administrative staff of
seven personnel. Annual purchasing volume was approximately
$50 million.

1975-1979:

Staff Assistant and Supply Systems Analyst, Office of the
Secretary of Defense, Installations and Logistics, the
Pentagon, Washington, D.C. Responsibilities included (1)
initial spare parts provisioning of new weapon systems and
equipment procurements, (2) development and monitoring of
retail level stockage policies, (3) review and approval of
supply program budgets for Defense Logistics Agency, (4)
development, implementation and monitoring of Department of
Defense (DOD) Food Service Program, and (5) participation in
the inter agency committee to revise the government-wide
procurement and distribution system for medical and
nonperishable subsistence items.

1974-1975:

Air Force representative to the DOD Retail Inventory
Management and Stockage Policy (RIMSTOP) Working Group.
Responsible for the development of standard management
policies and stockage criteria to control over $6 billion of
inventory required at the retail levels.

1972-1974:

Staff Supply Officer, Headquarters U.S. Air Force (Maintenance Engineering and Supply), the Pentagon, Washington, D.C. Responsible for the development and monitoring of supply policy for the Air Force.

1971-1972:

Graduate Student Air Force Institute of Technology. Graduated with distinction with M.S. degree in Logistics Management.

1958-1971:

Various assignments in the supply management and logistics area in the United States Air Force.

Personal Data:

- Member NIGP since 1980
- Member Board of Directors, NIGP since 1987
- Petitioner and President, Charleston Chapter
- Member West Virginia Association of Governmental Purchasing (WVAGP) Chapter since 1980.
- Chairman, West Virginia Council of Governments' Purchasing Officers Committee, 1983-1984
- Active instructor in NIGP Purchasing Management Courses
- Married, two children

1. The experience should be listed first. Follow with education.

2. The organization and position should be separated.

3. Rewrite with active verb. ①

4. Highlight this as an accomplishment.

5. This sounds like two positions and yet it is a promotion. Format in such a way that this is evident.

6. This is formatted differently than ② the other experiences. Be consistent.

Charles N. Taylor, CPPO   ⑨
75 Cedar Drive
Charleston, West Virginia 25305
304-788-3200 (H), 304-908-5500 (W)

Education:

> B.S. West Virginia University
> M.S. Logistics Management, Air Force Institute of Technology

Work History:

1980-Present:

Director, Purchasing and Supply Management Agency, Charleston County, West Virginia. Responsible for central purchasing for county government and school system, and supply management system for county governmental activities. Direct major agency ③ of over 50 personnel with annual purchasing volume in excess of $100 million. Responsible for development and ④ implementation of integrated purchasing and inventory management automated system.

1979-1980:   ⑤

Senior Buyer, West Virginia University, and Purchasing Manager for the University Medical Center. Responsible for planning, budgeting, and purchasing medical supplies, equipment, and services to support major medical center. Supervised a staff of two professional buyers and an administrative staff of seven personnel. Annual purchasing volume was approximately $50 million.

1975-1979:

Staff Assistant and Supply Systems Analyst, Office of the Secretary of Defense, Installations and Logistics, the Pentagon, Washington, D.C. Responsibilities included (1) ⑥ initial spare parts provisioning of new weapon systems and equipment procurements, (2) development and monitoring of retail level stockage policies, (3) review and approval of supply program budgets for Defense Logistics Agency, (4) development, implementation and monitoring of Department of Defense (DOD) Food Service Program, and (5) participation in the inter agency committee to revise the government-wide procurement and distribution system for medical and nonperishable subsistence items.

1974-1975:

Air Force representative to the DOD Retail Inventory Management and Stockage Policy (RIMSTOP) Working Group. Responsible for the development of standard management policies and stockage criteria to control over $6 billion of inventory required at the retail levels.

7. These can be combined.

8. Include the honors with education.

9. What do these mean?

10. Organize these better.

11. Eliminate.

(7)

1972-1974:

Staff Supply Officer, Headquarters U.S. Air Force (Maintenance Engineering and Supply), the Pentagon, Washington, D.C. Responsible for the development and monitoring of supply policy for the Air Force.

1971-1972:

(8)

Graduate Student Air Force Institute of Technology. Graduated with distinction with M.S. degree in Logistics Management.

1958-1971:

(7)

Various assignments in the supply management and logistics area in the United States Air Force.

Personal Data: (9)

- Member NIGP since 1980
- Member Board of Directors, NIGP since 1987
- Petitioner and President, Charleston Chapter
- Member West Virginia Association of Governmental Purchasing (WVAGP) Chapter since 1980.
- Chairman, West Virginia Council of Governments' Purchasing Officers Committee, 1983-1984
- Active instructor in NIGP Purchasing Management Courses
- Married, two children (11)

(10)

Comments: This résumé is difficult to read and understand. Position titles need to be emphasized to show career progression. This résumé can fit on one page.

CHARLES N. TAYLOR, CPPO
75 Cedar Drive
Charleston, West Virginia 25305
(304) 788-3200 (H) (304) 908-5500 (W)

EMPLOYMENT HISTORY

CHARLESTON COUNTY, Charleston, West Virginia
Director, Purchasing and Supply Management Agency, 1980 - present
Direct central purchasing agency for county government, school system, and supply management system for county governmental activities. Manage a staff of 50 and annual purchasing volume in excess of $100 million.

Designed and implemented an integrated and automated purchasing and inventory management system.

WEST VIRGINIA UNIVERSITY AND UNIVERSITY MEDICAL CENTER, Charleston, West Virginia
Purchasing Manager, 1980
Senior Buyer, 1979
Planned, budgeted, and purchased medical supplies, equipment, and services to support major medical center with an annual purchasing volume of approximately $50 million. Supervised a staff of two professional buyers and an administrative staff of seven personnel.

OFFICE OF THE SECRETARY OF DEFENSE, INSTALLATIONS AND LOGISTICS, Washington, D. C.
Supply Systems Analyst, 1978 - 1979
Staff Assistant, 1975 - 1978
Established and monitored retail level stockage policies and reviewed and approved supply program budgets for Defense Logistics Agency. Initiated, implemented, and monitored Department of Defense (DOD) Food Service Program. Handled initial spare parts provisioning of new weapon systems and equipment procurements. Participated in the inter agency committee to revise the government-wide procurement and distribution system for medical and nonperishable subsistence items.

DOD RETAIL INVENTORY MANAGEMENT AND STOCKAGE POLICY (RIMSTOP) WORKING GROUP, Washington, D. C.
Air Force Representative, 1974-1975
Developed standard management policies and stockage criteria to control over $6 billion in inventory required at the retail levels.

UNITED STATES AIR FORCE 1958-1974
Staff Supply Officer Headquarters, Maintenance Engineering and Supply, Washington, D. C. 1972-1974
Developed and monitored supply policy for the Air Force.

Various assignments in the supply management and logistic area. 1958-1971

EDUCATION

Master of Science, Logistics Management, Air Force Institute of Technology, Houston, Texas 1972
Graduated with distinction
Bachelor of Science, Business, West Virginia University, Charleston, West Virginia 1958

PROFESSIONAL ASSOCIATIONS

National Institute of Governmental Purchasing (NIGP) 1980 - present
Member, Board of Directors, 1987 - present
Petitioner and President, Charleston Chapter
Instructor in NIGP Purchasing Management Courses
West Virginia Association of Governmental Purchasing (WVAGP) 1980-present
Chairman, West Virginia Council of Governments' Purchasing Officers Committee, 1983-1984

PROFESSIONAL CERTIFICATION

Certified Professional Purchasing Officer

LYNNE PLANES

12 Hollywood Avenue, Eastchester, New York 10707   (914) 968-8357

Career Objective

A responsible and challenging position in the field of career development
and training.

Experience

Westchester County Office of Adult Education, White Plains, New York

Career Planning Program Specialist, 1983 - present

Coordinate and schedule career planning program for county adult education.
Develop courses, manage program, recruit, interview and hire instructors.
Designed career counseling program, developed alternative career workstyles,
entrepreneurship, career exploration and job hunting preparation.

Instructor, 1982 - present

Develop curriculum and teach Job Hunting Techniques, Résumés, Interviewing
Techniques, Job Leads, Networking, Part-Time Career Opportunities, Crossroads for Women, and the Professional Image.

GTE Telenet, Stamford, Connecticut

Technical Writer, 1983

Wrote administrative procedural manual for new billing system. Gathered
information through interviews, group meetings, and liaison with other
consultants. Designed binders, ordered supplies, coordinated typing,
proofing, copying and distribution of manual.

Xerox Corporation, Rosslyn, Virginia

District Billing Manager, 1979 - 1980

Managed billing department for five branch offices. Direct responsibility
for staff of ten; recruited, supervised, developed position descriptions,
created and utilized training material, established performance criteria
and appraised performance.

Office Services Supervisor, 1978 - 1979

Supervised administrative secretarial communication network for 22
secretaries supporting 200 managers. Established support position guides,
performance standards, and secretarial handbooks. Conducted awareness
seminars, team building workshops, and third party counseling.

Marriott Corporation, Bethesda, Maryland

Credit Manager, 1978

Managed credit department for Contract Food Services Division. Approved
credit, resolved billing and credit problems and collected outstanding
receivables. Staff of one.

Xerox of Canada, Toronto, Ontario

Customer Services Manager, 1975 - 1977

Developed and implemented credit and collection programs and maintained cash flows. Staff of seven.

Major Account Administrator, 1974 - 1975

Coordinated and implemented a new major account price plan; developed procedures, initiated changes in corporate policy, developed and gave administrative presentations to customers, sales, and administration.

Major Account Coordinator, 1973 - 1974

Initiated collection programs for major accounts. Resolved billing and collection problems.

Xerox Corporation, Syracuse, New York

Credit and Collection Correspondent, 1972 - 1973

Developed expertise in credit and collection procedures.

Education

George Mason University, Fairfax, Virginia

Bachelor of Arts, English. 1980.

York University, Toronto, Ontario

Attended 1973 - 1975.

Monroe Community College, Rochester, New York

Associate in Applied Arts, Liberal Arts. 1969.

Management Development at Xerox; Management Studies, New Manager Seminar, Managing for Motivation, Management Action Workshop.

Professional Affiliations

American Society of Training and Development
Association of Part-Time Professionals

1. Strengthen career objective.

2. What does the first experience have in common with the third? Is there a pattern of a progressive career path or increased responsibility?

3. What are the accomplishments?

4. These indicate a career change. The format makes it look as if the individual skipped around a lot.

LYNNE PLANES

12 Hollywood Avenue, Eastchester, New York 10707   (914) 968-8357

Career Objective

A responsible and challenging position in the field of career development and training.

Experience

Westchester County Office of Adult Education, White Plains, New York

Career Planning Program Specialist, 1983 - present

Coordinate and schedule career planning program for county adult education. Develop courses, manage program, recruit, interview and hire instructors. Designed career counseling program, developed alternative career workstyles, entrepreneurship, career exploration and job hunting preparation.

Instructor, 1982 - present

Develop curriculum and teach Job Hunting Techniques, Résumés, Interviewing Techniques, Job Leads, Networking, Part-Time Career Opportunities, Crossroads for Women, and the Professional Image.

GTE Telenet, Stamford, Connecticut

Technical Writer, 1983

Wrote administrative procedural manual for new billing system. Gathered information through interviews, group meetings, and liaison with other consultants. Designed binders, ordered supplies, coordinated typing, proofing, copying and distribution of manual.

Xerox Corporation, Rosslyn, Virginia

District Billing Manager, 1979 - 1980

Managed billing department for five branch offices. Direct responsibility for staff of ten; recruited, supervised, developed position descriptions, created and utilized training material, established performance criteria and appraised performance.

Office Services Supervisor, 1978 - 1979

Supervised administrative secretarial communication network for 22 secretaries supporting 200 managers. Established support position guides, performance standards, and secretarial handbooks. Conducted awareness seminars, team building workshops, and third party counseling.

Marriott Corporation, Bethesda, Maryland

Credit Manager, 1978

Managed credit department for Contract Food Services Division. Approved credit, resolved billing and credit problems and collected outstanding receivables. Staff of one.

5. Lack of emphasis causes one position to blend into the other.

6. Eliminate. Include the degrees only. This information takes away rather than adds.

7. These are highlighted the same even though these are different areas. There is a problem with distinction.

8. Too much white space.

⑤

Xerox of Canada, Toronto, Ontario

Customer Services Manager, 1975 - 1977

Developed and implemented credit and collection programs and maintained cash flows. Staff of seven.

Major Account Administrator, 1974 - 1975

Coordinated and implemented a new major account price plan; developed procedures, initiated changes in corporate policy, developed and gave administrative presentations to customers, sales, and administration.

Major Account Coordinator, 1973 - 1974

Initiated collection programs for major accounts. Resolved billing and collection problems.

Xerox Corporation, Syracuse, New York

Credit and Collection Correspondent, 1972 - 1973

Developed expertise in credit and collection procedures.

Education

George Mason University, Fairfax, Virginia

Bachelor of Arts, English. 1980.

⑧

York University, Toronto, Ontario

⑥ Attended 1973 - 1975.

Monroe Community College, Rochester, New York

Associate in Applied Arts, Liberal Arts. 1969.

⑦ Management Development at Xerox; Management Studies, New Manager Seminar, Managing for Motivation, Management Action Workshop.

Professional Affiliations

American Society of Training and Development
Association of Part-Time Professionals

Comments: The work experiences are fairly well written and yet this résumé does not work. The problem lies in the presentation. What we notice is an obvious shift in career direction rather than the experience. Chronological résumés work best with progressive career advancement. A functional résumé would more advantageously emphasize the skills and accomplishments and support the career objective.

LYNNE PLANES

12 Hollywood Avenue
Eastchester, New York 10707
(914) 968-8357

CAREER OBJECTIVE

A challenging training position in private industry, concentrating on management development and career planning

AREAS OF EFFECTIVENESS

Program Development/Administration

♦ Coordinate and schedule career planning for county adult education program. Develop courses, manage program, recruit, interview, and hire instructors. Experienced 102% growth in student enrollment. Increased course offerings by 50%.

♦ Designed a career counseling program, developed alternative career workstyles, entrepreneurship, career explorations, and job hunting preparation. Created programs with local high technology and health care industries, offering career exploration at the work site.

♦ Wrote administrative procedural manual for new billing system. Gathered information through interviews, group meetings, and liaison with other consultants. Designed binders, ordered supplies, coordinated typing, proofreading, copying, and distribution of manual.

♦ Coordinated and implemented a new major account price plan; developed procedures, initiated changes in corporate policy, developed and gave administrative presentations to customers, sales, and administration.

Training/Teaching

♦ Develop curriculum and teach training programs in Management Development, Job Hunting Techniques, Resume Writing, Interviewing Techniques, Job Leads, Part-Time Career Opportunities, Crossroads for Women, Networking, and the Professional Image.

♦ Research material; create handouts, reference tools, and bibliographies.

Management

♦ Direct responsibility for staffs of 7 to 22; recruited, supervised, developed position descriptions; created and utilized training material; established performance criteria and appraised performance.

♦ Managed billing department for machine population of 16,000 units and annual revenue of $66 million.

♦ Developed and implemented credit and collection programs and maintained cash flows for $33 million in annual revenue.

♦ Supervised administrative secretarial communication network for 22 secretaries supporting 200 managers. Established support position guides, performance standards, and secretarial handbooks. Conducted awareness seminars, team building workshops, and third party counseling.

EMPLOYMENT

✦ *Westchester County Schools*, White Plains, New York

    Career Planning Program Specialist, Office of Adult and Community Education, 1983-present
    Instructor, 1982-Present

✦ *GTE Telenet*, Stamford, Connecticut

    Technical Writer, 1983

✦ *Xerox Corporation*, Rosslyn, Virginia

    District Billing Manager, 1979–1980
    Office Services Supervisor, 1978–1979

✦ *Marriott Corporation*, Bethesda, Maryland

    Credit Manager, 1978

✦ *Xerox of Canada*, Ontario, Canada

    Customer Service Manager, 1975-1977
    Major Account Administrator, 1974-1975
    Major Account Coordinator, 1973-1974

✦ *Xerox Corporation*, Syracuse, New York

    Credit and Collection Correspondent, 1972-1973

EDUCATION

✦ *George Mason University*, Fairfax Virginia

    Bachelor of Arts, English, 1980

✦ *Monroe Community College*, Rochester, New York

    Associate in Applied Arts/Liberal Arts, 1969

✦ *Xerox Corporation Management Training*

    Management Studies, New Manager Seminar, Managing for Motivation, Management Action Workshop

PROFESSIONAL AFFILIATIONS

American Society for Training and Development
Association of Part-time Professionals

MRS. CLAUDIA WHITE   14 Linton Road
    Telephone: (301) 966-4000   Gaithersburg, MD. 20760

EXPERIENCE:

CAREER PERSONNEL   1982 to present
Gaithersburg, MD

Responsibilities: (in sequence)
Branch Manager – Hire, train, and supervise a staff of four.
Oversee all temporary recruitment and placement.
Recruiter – Established position to recruit temporary applicants.
    Accomplished this by considerable public speaking on employment
    topics.
Marketing Representative – Called on established clients and made
    cold calls to obtain new business and took job orders as needed.
Interviewer – Interviewed and tested temporary applicants, took and
    filled job orders, and performed quality control checks.

CHESEBOROUGH-POND'S INC.   1971 to 1973
Greenwich, CT

Responsibilities: (in sequence)
Personnel Secretary to the Employment Manager, Clerical Personnel –
    most agency contact, pre-screening and testing, scheduling of
    appointments.
Personnel Aide to Employment Manager – During this time company
    moved from N.Y. City to Greenwich and required over 50%
    replacement of the clerical staff. Involved establishing new
    agency contacts. As jobs opened, recruited applicants from Conn.
    able to work temporarily in N. Y. At the time of the move not a
    single job was unfilled.
Compensation Assistant – reported to Manager of Compensation &
    Benefits – upper level employment-termination papers, supervised
    payroll clerk, coordinated insurance benefits, EEOC reports,
    organizational charts, worked on Employee Bonus Plans, salary
    surveys and special reports.

EXECUTIVE RESEARCH INTERNATIONAL   1969 to 1970
New York, NY

Responsibilities: (in sequence)
Assistant Secretary – typing, filing and reception
General Secretary – supervision of receptionist and 3 part-time
    girls, typing, purchasing, accounts payable
Asst. to Placement Consultant – Same responsibilities as Gen.
    Secretary, with heavy client contact and reporting.
Administrative Assistant – coordination of printing and mailing of
    client marketplace, handling of newspaper advertising, invoices,
    purchasing, proofreading, and administering and scoring tests.

EDUCATION: B. A., 1969, University of Rochester, N. Y.
          Major: History   Special Emphasis on Latin America

133

1. Eliminate the marital status.

2. Eliminate "in sequence"—use dates to indicate sequence.

3. Don't abbreviate.

4. There's not very much information for current jobs. Elaborate more and emphasize accomplishments and contributions.

5. There is more information here from the 1970s than the present. This along with the following position could be summarized under "Related Experiences."

6. Once you have moved into management, downplay clerical skills from previous positions.

(1) MRS. CLAUDIA WHITE   14 Linton Road
    Telephone: (301) 966-4000   Gaithersburg, MD. 20760

EXPERIENCE:

CAREER PERSONNEL   1982 to present
Gaithersburg, MD (3)

Responsibilities: (in sequence) (2)
Branch Manager – Hire, train, and supervise a staff of four.
Oversee all temporary recruitment and placement.
(4) Recruiter – Established position to recruit temporary applicants.
    Accomplished this by considerable public speaking on employment
    topics.
Marketing Representative – Called on established clients and made
    cold calls to obtain new business and took job orders as needed.
Interviewer – Interviewed and tested temporary applicants, took and
    filled job orders, and performed quality control checks.

CHESEBOROUGH-POND'S INC.   1971 to 1973
Greenwich, CT   (3)

Responsibilities: (in sequence)
Personnel Secretary to the Employment Manager, Clerical Personnel –
    most agency contact, pre-screening and testing, scheduling of
    appointments.
(5) Personnel Aide to Employment Manager – During this time company
    moved from N.Y. City to Greenwich and required over 50%
    replacement of the clerical staff. Involved establishing new
    agency contacts. As jobs opened, recruited applicants from Conn.
    able to work temporarily in N. Y. At the time of the move not a
    single job was unfilled.
Compensation Assistant – reported to Manager of Compensation &
    Benefits - upper level employment-termination papers, supervised
    payroll clerk, coordinated insurance benefits, EEOC reports,
    organizational charts, worked on Employee Bonus Plans, salary
    surveys and special reports.

EXECUTIVE RESEARCH INTERNATIONAL   1969 to 1970
New York, NY (3)

Responsibilities: (in sequence)
Assistant Secretary – typing, filing and reception
General Secretary – supervision of receptionist and 3 part-time
    girls, typing, purchasing, accounts payable
(6) Asst. to Placement Consultant – Same responsibilities as Gen.
    Secretary, with heavy client contact and reporting.
Administrative Assistant – coordination of printing and mailing of
    client marketplace, handling of newspaper advertising, invoices,
    purchasing, proofreading, and administering and scoring tests.

EDUCATION: B. A., 1969, University of Rochester, N. Y.
          Major: History   Special Emphasis on Latin America

Comments: Some type of summary or objective is needed to tie this together. Emphasize current experiences unless the previous experience is particularly impressive. In this case, the current is more important.

CLAUDIA WHITE
14 Linton Road
Gaithersburg, Maryland 20760
(301) 966-4000 (H) (301) 964-7755 (B)

QUALIFICATIONS SUMMARY: 12 years of progressive experience in a variety of personnel positions. Frequent speaker/lecturer for academic, military, community, and governmental organizations.

EXPERIENCE

Career Personnel

BRANCH MANAGER, Gaithersburg, Maryland 1989 - present
Manage temporary placement agency. Hire, train, and supervise staff of four. Oversee all temporary recruitment, create promotional strategies to increase business; design, place, and monitor advertising; implement strategies to ensure client satisfaction and repeat business.

RECRUITER, Tysons Corner, Virginia 1985 - 1989
Established a position to recruit temporary and permanent applicants for four local offices. Developed a public relations program that provides speakers for local organizations on employment topics. Created an awareness of employment opportunities within Career Personnel

Research, develop, and present a wide range of speeches. Attend job fairs; visit college campuses, military recruiters, job support, senior, and women's groups; any additional organizations or employer contacts. Act as service coordinator to meet office needs.

MARKETING REPRESENTATIVE, Gaithersburg, Maryland 1984 - 1985
Coordinated customer relations with established clientele in the Gaithersburg and Frederick area. Obtained new business through cold calls.

INTERVIEWER, Gaithersburg, Maryland 1982 - 1984
Interviewed and tested temporary applicants, assessed employers needs, and filled job orders. Contacted employers for follow-up to determine customer satisfaction.

Association of Part-Time Professionals

SPEAKER, McLean, Virginia 1987 - present
Developed a speech on part-time career opportunities and deliver as needed. Act as spokesperson for the organization in interviews for magazines, newspapers, and cable television.

RELATED EXPERIENCES

Cheseborough-Pond's Inc., Greenwich, Connecticut 1971 - 1973
Progressive promotions to Assistant to Employment Manager. Established new agency contacts, prescreened prospective employees, tested applicants, and interfaced with all levels of management. Supervised staff of one.

Executive Research International, New York, New York 1969 - 1970
Progressive promotions to Administrative Assistant. Supervised the printing and mailing of client resumes, placed newspaper advertisements, and administered and scored psychological tests.

EDUCATION

Bachelor of Arts in History, University of Rochester, Rochester, New York, 1969

VALERIE WEIL

25 Court Street
Madison, Wisconsin 76805
Home Phone: (502) 886-0944
Work Phone: (502) 883-1614

CAREER OBJECTIVE

A position as an Administrative Assistant that is challenging and will
lead to greater opportunity and more responsibility.

EDUCATION

1986 Katharine Gibbs School, Madison, Wisconsin
     Administrative Assistant Program

1984 Katharine Gibbs School, Madison, Wisconsin
     Entree Program

1978 - 1983 University of Wisconsin, Madison, Wisconsin
            Bachelor of Arts in elementary education

WORK EXPERIENCE

Secretary: Association of Airline Transportation (AAT) - 1986
I worked in the capacity of secretary in the Air Traffic
Management Department where I worked for a director and
two managers with duties that included: organizing conferences and meetings, being responsible for record management, prioritizing assignments, implementing ideas
and strategies daily, familiarity with Wang word processor,
use of facsimile machine, and the ability to send wires.

Secretary: Reporting Corporation of Airlines (RCA) - 1984 - 1986
Here I worked in the Financial Recovery Department where
I worked under a single manager. My responsibilities included: composing correspondences, providing input regarding policies for office management created and was responsible for record management, coordinated and compiled diverse
information (semi-annual report), trained staff and explained
concepts, took dictation, handled financial aspects such as,
checks and letters of credits, composed and sent memo of agency
termination, paid-in-full or bankruptcy claims, and handled
telephone correspondences.

Assistant Teacher: Madison's Child Development Center - 1983 - 1984
Here I was an assistant teacher to the 3, 4, and 5
year olds. My responsibilities included: supervising
the children in their play, projects, and learning
skills.

1. Eliminate the word "phone."

2. It's fine to look for opportunity and responsibility—by rephrasing "more responsibility and greater opportunity" it sounds less self serving.

3. Combine these two.

4. Present experience should be in present tense—not past.

5. Awkward sentence structure and run-on sentences.

6. Correspondence is already plural and does not take an "s".

7. Wordy. Use active verbs.

8. Awkward sentence—Eliminate first four words.

9. Too heavy.

10. Don't use pronouns.

VALERIE WEIL

25 Court Street
Madison, Wisconsin 76805
(1) Home Phone: (502) 886-0944
Work Phone: (502) 883-1614

CAREER OBJECTIVE

(2) A position as an Administrative Assistant that is challenging and will lead to greater opportunity and more responsibility.

EDUCATION

1986 Katharine Gibbs School, Madison, Wisconsin
(3)   Administrative Assistant Program

1984 Katharine Gibbs School, Madison, Wisconsin
     Entree Program

1978 - 1983 University of Wisconsin, Madison, Wisconsin
     Bachelor of Arts in elementary education

WORK EXPERIENCE

Secretary: Association of Airline Transportation (AAT) - 1986
(4) I worked in the capacity of secretary in the Air Traffic Management Department where I worked for a director and
(9) two managers with duties that included: organizing conferences and meetings, being responsible for record management, prioritizing assignments, implementing ideas and strategies daily, familiarity with Wang word processor, use of facsimile machine, and the ability to send wires.

(10) Secretary: Reporting Corporation of Airlines (RCA) - 1984 - 1986
Here I worked in the Financial Recovery Department where I worked under a single manager. My responsibilities in- (5)
cluded: composing correspondences, providing input regarding policies for office management created and was respon-
(9) sible for record management, coordinated and compiled diverse information (semi-annual report), trained staff and explained concepts, took dictation, handled financial aspects such as, checks and letters of credits, composed and sent memo of agency termination, paid-in-full or bankruptcy claims, and handled telephone correspondences. (6)

Assistant Teacher: Madison's Child Development Center - 1983 - 1984
(8) Here I was an assistant teacher to the 3, 4, and 5 year olds. My responsibilities included: supervising (7) the children in their play, projects, and learning skills.

Comments: Skills need to be highlighted. Writing is a awkward and overshadows the experience. Uneven white space. Not easy to read. Experience needs to support career objective.

VALERIE WEIL

25 Court Street, Madison, Wisconsin 768005

(502) 886-0944 (Home)
(502) 883-1614 (Work)

Career Objective

An administrative position that is challenging and will lead to greater responsibility and opportunity.

Skills

- Typewriting, 70 words per minute.
- Shorthand, 50 words per minute.
- Word processing training on IBM Displaywriter and Wang VS-85 System.
- Ability to operate dictaphone and facsimile machine.

Education

Katharine Gibbs School, Madison, Wisconsin
Administrative Assistant Program, 1986.
Entree Program, 1984.

University of Wisconsin, Madison, Wisconsin
Bachelor of Arts in Elementary Education, 1983.

Experience

Secretary, Association of Airline Transportation (AAT), Madison, Wisconsin.
1986–present

Support director and two managers in the Air Traffic Management Department. Organize conferences and meetings, create and maintain file systems, prioritize assignments and implement ideas and strategies. Familiar with Wang word processor, use of facsimile machine, and the ability to send wires.

Secretary, Reporting Corporation of Airlines (RCA), Madison, Wisconsin.
1984–1986

Secretary to manager of Financial Recovery Department. Composed correspondence, provided input regarding policies for office management, created and was responsible for record management. Coordinated and compiled diverse information (semi-annual reports), trained staff and explained concepts. Coordinated financial aspects such as checks and letters of credit from travel agencies, communicated and updated agency terminations, accounts and bankruptcy claims and handled telephone correspondence.

Assistant Teacher, Madison's Child Development Center, Madison, Wisconsin.
1983–1984

Supervised 25 pre-school children in their learning skills, projects and recreation.

Associate Memberships

World Airlines Clubs Association
National Trust for Historic Preservation

Louise J. Silver
89 Kings Park Ridge
Evans, Oregon 09422
(717) 894-0700 (h)
(717) 544-8722 (w)

RESUME

Special Educator

GENERAL BACKGROUND AND SKILLS

Eight years of experience in the field of special education; diagnosis
and remediation of specific learning disabilities, development and
implementation of specialized curriculum for the mentally retarded,
program modification for students with learning disabilities, kindergarten readiness testing. Strong organizational and communication
skills.

EXPERIENCE

1981 - present   Young Adult Institute, Evans and Buhl, Oregon
                     Program Resource Specialist

Responsibilities include development of curriculum, co-leading specialty
groups, evaluating appropriateness of programming through the Utilization
Review process, program compliance with state regulations. Developed
systems for record keeping. Established student internship program with
local colleges. Developed and carried out Program Evaluation system and
Community Education/Outreach program. Responsible for writing and submission of grant proposals. Direct care with profound MR. multiple-
handicapped adults.

1980 - 1981   Allegheny Central School, Allegheny, Oregon
                     Special Teaching Assignment

Teacher for homebound profoundly retarded child. Responsibilities
included developing and carrying out daily program instruction and
home management. Skills stressed included sustained eye contact,
grasp, balance, awareness of sounds, touch, and self.

1980 - 1981   BOCES, Buhl, Oregon (Evans Central School)
                     Teacher for Resource Room

Responsibilities included development of program goals. Diagnosed and
remediated specific disabilities; recommended program modifications for
students in mainstream classes. Prepared students for RCT in reading,
writing, and mathematics.

1976 - 1980   BOCES, Allegheny and Evans Central Schools
                     Temporary and Substitute Teacher

Long-term assignments in primary grades; developed teaching strategies
and modified curriculum for disadvantaged children. Substituted in all
grades in elementary school and special education classes for the trainable and educable mentally retarded.

CERTIFICATION   Special Classes of the Mentally Retarded and N-6
                     Permanent, Oregon

EDUCATION   M. S., Education; Oregon State
                     B. S., Education & Behavioral Science, Mercy College,
                     Evans, Oregon

1. Omit. This looks as if it was copied from a book and the page heading was included.

2. The purpose of this area is to emphasize skills. When the paragraph is heavy and not easy to read—this defeats the purpose.

3. Too wordy. Lacks authority.

4. Shift in tense.

5. Spell this out.

6. Redundant. Too many redundancies take away from the skills and accomplishments. "Developed" is used seven times!

7. Wordy and redundant.

8. This work location and the one below are not consistent with the first two.

9. What is this?

10. Where is the school located?

11. These two schools and degrees should be formatted the same.

12. Don't abbreviate the degrees.

13. Wordy. Use active verbs.

14. Heavy paragraphs are not easy to read.

Louise J. Silver
89 Kings Park Ridge
Evans, Oregon 09422
(717) 894-0700 (h)
(717) 544-8722 (w)

RESUME (1)

Special Educator

GENERAL BACKGROUND AND SKILLS

(2) (14) Eight years of experience in the field of special education; diagnosis and remediation of specific learning disabilities, development and implementation of specialized curriculum for the mentally retarded, program modification for students with learning disabilities, kindergarten readiness testing. Strong organizational and communication skills.

EXPERIENCE

1981 – present   Young Adult Institute, Evans and Buhl, Oregon
(3)   Program Resource Specialist

(13) Responsibilities include development of curriculum, co-leading specialty groups, evaluating appropriateness of programming through the Utilization Review process, program compliance with state regulations. Developed (4) systems for record keeping. Established student internship program with (6) local colleges. Developed and carried out Program Evaluation system and Community Education/Outreach program. Responsible for writing and submission of grant proposals. Direct care with profound MR. multiple-handicapped adults.

(5)

1980 – 1981   Allegheny Central School, Allegheny, Oregon
(8)   Special Teaching Assignment

Teacher for homebound profoundly retarded child. Responsibilities (7) included developing and carrying out daily program instruction and home management. Skills stressed included sustained eye contact, grasp, balance, awareness of sounds, touch, and self.

1980 – 1981   BOCES, Buhl, Oregon (Evans Central School)
                             Teacher for Resource Room

(13) Responsibilities included development of program goals. Diagnosed and remediated specific disabilities; recommended program modifications for students in mainstream classes. Prepared students for RCT in reading, writing, and mathematics.

(9)

1976 – 1980   BOCES, Allegheny and Evans Central Schools
                             Temporary and Substitute Teacher

Long-term assignments in primary grades; developed teaching strategies and modified curriculum for disadvantaged children. Substituted in all grades in elementary school and special education classes for the trainable and educable mentally retarded.

CERTIFICATION   Special Classes of the Mentally Retarded and N-6
                                 Permanent, Oregon

EDUCATION   (11) M. S., Education; Oregon State   (10)
                          B. S., Education & Behavioral Science, Mercy College,
                          (12) Evans, Oregon

Comments: This résumé is wordy and lacks authority. This is a highly skilled and trained individual and yet this doesn't come across. Experience and skills need to be developed and presented clearly.

LOUISE J. SILVER

89 Kings Park Ridge
Evans, Oregon 09422

(717) 894-0700 (h)
(717) 544-8722 (w)

—CAREER HISTORY—

- Eight years of experience in special education.
- Diagnosis and remediation of specific learning disabilities.
- Development and implementation of specialized curriculum for mentally retarded.
- Program modification for students with learning disabilities.

—EXPERIENCE—

Program Resource Specialist

Young Adult Institute, Evans and Buhl, Oregon   1981–present

Ensure compliance with state regulations for day treatment program for 270 mild to profoundly mentally retarded multiply handicapped adults. Design curriculum, co-lead specialty groups, and evaluate program appropriateness through Utilization Review Process. Write and submit grant proposals.

Established student internship program with local colleges, created and implemented Program Evaluation system and Community Education/Outreach program. Administered direct care. Devised systems for record keeping.

Special Teaching Assignment

Allegheny Central School, Allegheny, Oregon   1980–1981

Teacher for home-bound profoundly mentally retarded child. Established a daily program of instruction and home management. Stressed skills in sustained eye contact, grasp, balance, awareness of sounds, touch, and self.

Resource Room Teacher

BOCES, Evans Central School, Buhl, Oregon   1980–1981

Developed program goals and recommended program modifications for students in mainstream classes. Diagnosed and remediated specific disabilities. Prepared students for Regional Competency Test (RCT) in reading, writing, and mathematics.

Temporary and Substitute Teacher

BOCES, Allegheny and Evans Central Schools, Buhl, Oregon   1976–1980

Long-term assignments in primary grades. Planned teaching strategies and modified curriculum for disadvantaged children. Substituted in all grades in elementary school and special classes for the trainable and educable mentally retarded.

—CERTIFICATION—

Special Classes of the Mentally Retarded and N–6—Permanent, Oregon

—EDUCATION—

Master of Science in Education
Oregon State University, Corvallis, Oregon, 1970.

Bachelor of Science in Education and Behavioral Science
Mercy College, Evans, Oregon, 1967.

Bill Henry Thomas
54 Moon Lane
New City, Virginia 23456
H-703-340-9807

WORK EXPERIENCE

January 1985   Salesman/Delivery, The Transmission Service
to   New City, Virginia
Present

Duties include selling products to customers,
picking up orders from distribution center, and
delivering products to customer.

March 1982   Administrative Manager, Peterson-Jay and Associates
to   New City, Virginia
September 1984

Responsible for operation of personnel office.
U. S. and international travel for the purpose
of purchasing products for African countries as
well as the U. S. Met with key decision-makers
to meet this goal.

January 1981   Salesman, John Hancock Life Insurance
to   New City, Virginia
October 1981

Sold and wrote life insurance policies for customers,
met with customers on routine basis in order to review
existing policies, and maintained all insurance records.

June 1963   Personnel and Industrial Relations Superintendent.
to   Mobil Oil Operating Company.
July 1980   Cape Town, South Africa

Responsible for the field of labor relations, personnel
matters for the entire company consisting of 4,000 employees, management/government relations; 1963-1964 -
Workshop Brake rebuilder; 1964-1969 - Industrial Relations Officer; 1969 - two months on-the-job training
U. S. Steel Corporation, PA and participated with
their management team in negotiations with the Labor
Unions. 1969-1973 - Industrial Relations Section
Head; 1973-1974 - Assistant to Management; 1974-
1978 - Industrial Relations Superintendent; 1978-
1980 - Consultant to Management on Industrial Relations
matters.

Headed negotiations team regarding labor union agreement
between Mobil Oil Operating Company and Labor Union of
South Africa from 1973-1978.

Annual attendance to the International Labor Organization in Geneva, Switzerland from 1970-1980, participated
in month-long meeting representing the Employers of
South Africa.

142

September 1956 to April 1961	Driver, <u>Armstrong Rubber Company</u> Chicago, Illinois
	Delivered tires to customers. Was responsible for clerical duties including filing, typing, and answering phone.

EDUCATION

B. A. Liberal Arts, University of Cape Town, Cape Town, South Africa, 1950-1954

University of Chicago, Chicago, Illinois, 1956-1959, English, Philosophy, Labor Relations.

Kennedy University, Kent, Ohio, January 1969-June 1969. Received Certificate in Management and Labor Relations. Courses studied include Management, Labor, English and Business. One month on-the-job training with U. S. Steel Corporation, Pittsburgh, PA.

PERSONAL

Birth Date: January 19, 1933
Marital Status: Married, three children
Health: Excellent

1. This is not necessary. If only one phone number is included, it would be assumed to be the home number.

2. Wordy. Use action verbs.

3. What were the results?

4. Unclear. Did you participate in month-long meeting once or one month each year from 1970–1980?

5. 1. Too much important information in one large paragraph. 2. Inconsistent with the rest of experience. The other experience begins at most recent and works backward. This one begins with the oldest and works forward. This is in reverse.

6. This is confusing. Is this what the organization does?

7. The dates take up too wide a margin. Months are not necessary.

Bill Henry Thomas
54 Moon Lane
New City, Virginia 23456
(1) H-703-340-9807

WORK EXPERIENCE

January 1985
to
Present

(2)

Salesman/Delivery, The Transmission Service
New City, Virginia

Duties include selling products to customers, picking up orders from distribution center, and delivering products to customer.

(7) March 1982
to
September 1984

Administrative Manager, Peterson-Jay and Associates
New City, Virginia

Responsible for operation of personnel office. (6) U. S. and international travel for the purpose of purchasing products for African countries as well as the U. S. Met with key decision-makers to meet this goal.

January 1981
to
October 1981

Salesman, John Hancock Life Insurance
New City, Virginia

Sold and wrote life insurance policies for customers, met with customers on routine basis in order to review existing policies, and maintained all insurance records.

June 1963
to
July 1980

Personnel and Industrial Relations Superintendent.
Mobil Oil Operating Company.
Cape Town, South Africa

(5) Responsible for the field of labor relations, personnel matters for the entire company consisting of 4,000 employees, management/government relations; 1963-1964 – Workshop Brake rebuilder; 1964-1969 – Industrial Relations Officer; 1969 – two months on-the-job training U. S. Steel Corporation, PA and participated with their management team in negotiations with the Labor Unions. 1969-1973 – Industrial Relations Section Head; 1973-1974 – Assistant to Management; 1974-1978 – Industrial Relations Superintendent; 1978-1980 – Consultant to Management on Industrial Relations matters.

(3) Headed negotiations team regarding labor union agreement between Mobil Oil Operating Company and Labor Union of South Africa from 1973-1978.

Annual attendance to the International Labor Organization in Geneva, Switzerland from 1970-1980, participated (4) in month-long meeting representing the Employers of South Africa.

144

8. Repeat of the name and page number are not necessary. Staple a two page résumé.

9. This information is so far in the past it can be eliminated as it does not tie in or add to the career direction.

10. Spell out "Bachelor of Arts." Do not include the years attended— only the year of graduation.

11. Omit personal information. Include citizenship.

⑧ Bill Henry Thomas -- 2

⑨

September 1956 to April 1961	Driver, <u>Armstrong Rubber Company</u> Chicago, Illinois

Delivered tires to customers. Was responsible for clerical duties including filing, typing, and answering phone.

<u>EDUCATION</u>

⑩ B. A. Liberal Arts, University of Cape Town, Cape Town, South Africa, 1950-1954

University of Chicago, Chicago, Illinois, 1956-1959, English, Philosophy, Labor Relations.

Kennedy University, Kent, Ohio, January 1969-June 1969. Received Certificate in Management and Labor Relations. Courses studied include Management, Labor, English and Business. One month on-the-job training with U. S. Steel Corporation, Pittsburgh, PA.

⑪ <u>PERSONAL</u>

Birth Date: January 19, 1933
Marital Status: Married, three children
Health: Excellent

Comments: No career objective or career summary. The résumé gives no clue to the position that this individual is seeking. Content is weak. What are the skills and accomplishments? Too much white space.

BILL HENRY THOMAS

54 Moon Lane
New City, Virginia 23456
(703) 340-9807

EXECUTIVE EXPERIENCE IN PERSONNEL AND LABOR RELATIONS

Personnel

Managed and directed personnel office for company of 4,000 employees. Direct responsibility for staff of 25 including 3 section heads.

Oversaw recruiting, interviewing, employee benefits, and preparation of wage and salary scales.

Reviewed all grievances. Decided cases and took corrective action through suspension, warnings, and termination.

Kept employees informed of corporate news and policies through newsletter and radio station.

Created employee job descriptions; ensured fair hiring practices.

Labor Relations

Negotiated with labor unions on the terms and conditions that affected employees. Utilized current financial information on corporate stability and cost of living index.

Ensured terms and conditions of union management agreement were in force; kept management abreast of new labor laws.

Corporate representative at International Labor Organization (ILO) in Geneva, Switzerland for 11 years and at Labor Ministry.

Handled 25 labor agreements. Negotiated and settled five strikes—50% less strikes than previous administration.

Marketing

Arranged purchases for 15–20 African countries; researched and contacted manufacturers of specific consumer goods, negotiated lowest rates, and secured line of credit.

Marketed product from the initial sale, secured product from inventory, and delivered.

Sold, wrote, and reviewed life insurance policies.

EDUCATION

Certificate in Management and Labor Relations.
Kennedy University, Kent, Ohio. 1969.
Internship in U.S. Labor Union Negotiations.
U.S. Steel Corporation, Pittsburgh, Pennsylvania. 1969.
Bachelor of Arts in Liberal Arts.
University of Cape Town, Cape Town, South Africa. 1954.

CITIZENSHIP

United States

3 The Great Cover-up— Or How to Write Those Letters

The Cover Story

The cover letter introduces you to a prospective employer. A good introduction entices the reader to review your résumé. A well-written letter and carefully prepared résumé represent your best chance of making it to the next phase of the employment process—the job interview.

A good cover letter takes no more time to type than a weak letter—and both cost the same to mail. Furthermore, time you spend writing a good letter may pay off many times as standard phrases and means of expressing your interests and qualifications can be used again in other cover letters.

Cover letters fall into three categories:

1. Unsolicited letter.
2. Letters resulting from a referral or some contact.
3. Letter responding to a job advertisement.

The ability to communicate is an important quality employers seek in job candidates. View letter writing as an opportunity for you to show an employer your own skills in written communication. The accompanying figures demonstrate proper formats for a cover letter and the different parts.

Format

The most appropriate letter formats are the full block and the semiblock (sometimes called modified).

Full Block

_____
_____
_____

_____
_____
_____

_____ :

All of the typing is lined up against the left hand margin.

_____
_____

_____
_____

_____ ,

_____

Semiblock

_____
_____
_____

_____
_____
_____

_____ :

The address of the writer and the date are indented. The complimentary close and the writer's name are indented and lined up with the above.

_____
_____

_____
_____

_____ ,
_____

Parts of a Letter

Writer's address Date	10905 Willowbrook Lane Tulsa, Oklahoma 73110 October 17, 1987

Dr. Catherine VanArsdale
Manager of Employee Relations
Blackbeard Creamery
450 N Lincoln Street
Oklahoma City, OK 74110

> Inside address. Same as on envelope. Includes name, title, organization, street or box address, city, state, and zip code.

Dear Dr. VanArsdale:

> Salutation. Always begin with "Dear" followed by courtesy title and individual's last name.

Your recent ad in the **Tulsa Chronicle** . . .

My studies at the University of Oklahoma . . .

During summer vacations while in college . . .

You will find a résumé of my qualifications . . .

I will be in Oklahoma City on . . .

> Body of letter, single space, skip a line between paragraphs.

> Complimentary close, use "Sincerely," "Sincerely yours," or "Yours truly."

Sincerely,

Richard Talbot

Richard Talbot

> Always sign letter. Type your name under signature.

RT/lht

> Stenographic identification. Use if letter was typed for you. Your initials in caps, typist in lower case.

Enclosure

> Use "Enclosure" or "Encl." when you are enclosing a copy of your résumé.

Twenty Tips

1. Type each letter individually. Use an electric typewriter, word processor, or word processing software. If you can't do it yourself, ask a friend or hire a word processing or secretarial service.

2. Address the employing officer by name and, if possible, by title. Research names in the library or call the company. With so many organizational changes these days, it never hurts to call the organization to verify who is presently in the position and double-check the spelling and title.

3. Catch the employer's attention by opening your letter with a strong statement. An employer receives hundreds of letters a month and you want yours to be one that is read.

4. Keep your letter short. It should be one page with five to six paragraphs. It will hold the employer's interest and save you substantial time and cost in typing.

5. Use the center of your letter to arouse the employer's curiosity by stating brief facts about your experience and accomplishments.

6. State your contributions so the individual you are addressing will feel that hiring you will lead to higher production, greater efficiency, or better sales in their organization. If you've done it for one organization, you can do it for another.

7. Keep the tone of your letter positive and upbeat.

8. Be direct in requesting an interview or state that you will call to arrange a meeting. Letters should ask for something, and the most common thing to request is an interview.

9. Sign and date your cover letter.

10. Use right-hand justification for even right-hand margins. Electronic typewriters, word processors, and personal computers with word processing software offer justification where lines are automatically spaced to provide an even right-hand margin.

11. If you don't know a woman's preference when using a courtesy title, use Ms. If you are unable to determine the gender of an individual, omit the courtesy title.
    For example:

Leslie A. Jones
Dear Leslie A. Jones:

12. Use "Dear Employer:" when responding to a classified advertisement that doesn't give an individual's name. This courtesy title is very positive as it implies that the recipient will be your employer. It resolves the gender problem and eliminates the old fashioned Madam, Sir, or Gentlemen.

13. Use a 9½″ × 4⅛″ business-size envelope. The envelope

should be the same color and weight of the enclosed paper. Include a return address on the front of the envelope.

14. The outside address should always be the same as the reader's inside address. Justify all lines of the address on the left.

15. The state can be abbreviated both on the inside address of your letter and the outside address of your envelope. Use the acceptable post office abbreviations.

16. Never photocopy a cover letter. It gives the impression that you don't care and don't want to take the time to do it properly.

17. Check and recheck for spelling and typing mistakes. Remember that your letter represents you. A good presentation equals a good image.

18. Plan on mailing a group of letters all at the same time. If you will be mailing 50 letters and you think it will take you one month to complete all 50, date the letters all with the future completion date. When all the letters are completed, mail them. It is too confusing to follow them up if they have been mailed randomly. Also, if you are to receive three job offers, you want them to occur at the same time so that you may judge which is best for you.

19. When mailing a group of letters, prepare one for yourself and mail it with the others. You will have a good idea that the employer has received the letter when you receive yours. Add one day or two to allow it to travel through the organization's mail room before you follow up.

20. When mailing a batch of letters, or even one, try to think of when your letter will arrive so as to receive maximum attention. Most employers receive their heaviest mail on Mondays. On Fridays they may be more concerned with winding up the week rather than investigating new employees. Mail your letter so that it will arrive in employer offices on a Tuesday, Wednesday, or Thursday.

Unsolicited Letters

Unsolicited letters need to be appealing and well written. Ensure that you direct your letter to the appropriate individual. Double-check the spelling of the organization and the individual's name. Here are some tips:

1. Begin with a specific statement concerning the marketplace.
2. Highlight your most marketable skills.
3. State your most recent experience.
4. State your most recent accomplishments.
5. Plan a follow-up.
6. Close your letter on a positive and assertive note. "I look forward to speaking with you" because I know that I will be

speaking with you. An inappropriate or passive close would be "I hope to speak with you" or "I am anxious to speak with you." The former is too passive and the latter is too eager.

See the sample of an unsolicited letter from Patrick Kelly.

22 Waverly Street
Denver, CO 44521
January 9, 1987

Mr. William K. Smith
Controller
Atlas Construction
930 First Highway
Denver, CO 44235

Dear Mr. Smith:

Efficient and effective administration of sales and customer service support means good customer relations. Satisfied customers generate more business. I can contribute to your organization's effectiveness by establishing good working relations with customers and personnel at all organizational levels.

My experience during the past eight years of my career has developed skills in:

- organization
- communication
- problem solving
- goal setting

Most recently these skills have been put to use in a multinational corporation developing and implementing collection programs to maintain favorable cash flows, ensuring the validity of customer billings, and administering customer care programs.

Last year, under my direction, my branch exceeded all credit and collection targets and achieved a days sales outstanding of 28 days. My enclosed résumé highlights these accomplishments.

Mr. Smith, I will be calling you sometime during the next five days to discuss with you how my skills can be put to use at Atlas Construction.

I look forward to speaking with you.

Yours truly,

Patrick Kelly

Patrick Kelly

Enclosure

Letters Resulting From a Contact or Referral

The letter needs to be addressed to the individual you have contacted or been referred to. Mention the previous contact or referral in the first paragraph. Do not rely on someone to remember a previous conversation or meeting.

Keep these tips in mind:

1. As you remind the reader about a previous contact or referral, take this opportunity to say something positive about the organization or the position.
2. State those experiences that highlight skills that qualify you as a prospective candidate.
3. State your recent accomplishments.
4. Close your letter assertively, indicating that you will take the initiative to phone for an appointment.

See the sample of a letter from a contact from Carl Boswell.

42 Palm Road
Miami, FL 23079
May 13, 1989

Dr. Janet Merlino
Dean of Business
Dade Junior College
32 Grenada Boulevard
Miami, FL 32079

Dear Dr. Merlino:

David Fields, senior partner with Wilson, Fields and Brooks, has told me you have an opening for an instructor in your accounting program. My review of the curriculum suggests to me that my background could very well be of interest to you.

I hold a Master of Science degree in Accounting and am a Certified Public Accountant. My ten-year career in public accounting has included clients in both the public and private sector. My background includes two years teaching Introduction to Accounting and Auditing with Dade County Adult Education and as a guest lecturer at the University of Miami. Details appear on the attached résumé.

I will phone for an appointment and look forward to meeting you.

Sincerely yours,

Carl Boswell

Carl Boswell, CPA

Enclosure

Letters for a Job Advertisement

A letter responding to a job advertisement should follow the basic rules of good cover letter writing. When I was recruiting, we often received over 1,000 résumés in response to a classified job advertisement. How will your letter compete in a stack of 1,000? Make sure you open with an imaginative sentence and draw the reader's attention. These suggestions may help.

1. State the job for which you are applying and where you saw it advertised.
2. Ensure that all of your paragraphs don't begin with pronouns, particularly "I."
3. Comment on the qualifications listed in the advertisement.
4. Match your skills to the required qualifications.
5. State your interest in the job.
6. Carefully respond to all elements of the job or provide all requested information.

See the example of a letter from Regina Goslind.

HELP WANTED

CIRCULATION
SUBSCRIPTION ASSISTANT

Resp. for promotional follow up in subscriptions, through telemarketing & mailings. Req. 1 yr. exper. in telemarketing. Exper. in sales promotion & clerical pos. also helpful.

Send cover letter & résumé to: Mr. Rice, Personnel Mgr., Oshkosh Publications, 67 Ash St., Oshkosh, WI 87009. No phone calls or drop-ins please.

---

89 Seymour Way
Oshkosh, WI 87009
June 6, 1989

Mr. Bill Rice
Personnel Manager
Oshkosh Publications
67 Ash Street
Oshkosh, WI 87009

Dear Mr. Rice:

Communication skills are the key to success for the Subscription Assistant position you advertised in Wednesday's Herald Dispatch.

My expertise in the following areas qualifies me for this position:

- Excellent oral and written communication skills.
- Two years of telemarketing experience with the Associated Press.
- One year of experience promoting a local weekly publication.
- One year of clerical experience in a retail operation.
- An Associates degree in Liberal Arts with an English major.

The Subscription Assistant position is in line with my career goals, as outlined in my enclosed résumé. I would like to meet with you and discuss how I will be able to contribute to your organization.

Sincerely,

Regina Goslind

Regina Goslind

Encl.

4 The Undercover Story—Letters From the Experts

You won't need detective skills to locate the best cover letters. My investigation led me to the experts, top personnel managers. To find out what they wanted in a cover letter, I asked them to respond to job openings and write their own letters. The following section highlights job openings and cover letters written by the experts—as they would like to see them written.*

In each example, a top personnel manager has chosen a job announcement or advertisement. What follows is a cover letter each has written to apply for the job opening. Read them yourself and learn different approaches that you can utilize in presenting your qualifications effectively.

---

*Please note: In no way do the following organizations endorse or guarantee that you will get a response from their organization using a particular cover letter format.

ART DIRECTOR

LOW 50's

The New York Times is seeking an art director to oversee our promotion art department.

Job responsibilities include the supervision of fifteen designers and mechanical artists, overall direction for all print and emerging computer graphic art promotion work, budget, and job traffic management.

Applicants should have at least five years of managerial experience with publication design and art direction. In addition, candidates should have excellent communication and administrative skills and be able to work well with editors and marketing ad sales personnel.

Salary (plus incentives) and benefits are excellent.

If interested, send resume and salary history in confidence to:

Brenda Watson

The New York Times

229 West 43rd St.
New York, N.Y. 10036
An Equal Opportunity Employer

The New York Times
Brenda Watson, Director, Recruiting and Employment

Ms. Brenda Watson
The New York Times
229 West 43rd Street
New York, NY 10036

Dear Ms. Watson:

In response to your advertisement in The Times for an Art Director, I am enclosing my résumé for your consideration.

I am thoroughly experienced in all phases of graphic design and communication.

In my present position, I manage a staff of ten designers and have responsibility for designing and directing the production of diverse projects to promote the company's image and position. These projects are in the form of sales promotions, recruiting brochures, personnel information and training publications, announcements, corporate publications, management meeting materials, and other corporate literature.

My corporate experience and demonstrated ability to work well with others to control project quality and cost will be of value to the position.

I hope that after you review the attached résumé, we can meet to discuss the position further. You may reach me at work (212-798-0000) or home (212-777-0000).

Thank you for your time and I look forward to hearing from you.

Sincerely,

PRICING ANALYST
POSITION DESCRIPTION

Major Responsibilities:

— Develop pricing proposals encompassing market and financial analysis
— Prepare and deliver implementation materials for approved pricing actions
— Interface effectively with Marketing, Finance, Service and Administration, and Systems departments, to ensure concurrence, implementation, and systems support for proposed actions
— Develop financial plans and on-going outlook assessments for activity, price, and profit levels

Qualifications and Experience:

— Previous analytical experience
— University degree in Business or Commerce preferred
— Strong analytical skills
— Excellent communications and interpersonal skills
— Ability to work in very dynamic environment
— Lots of initiative

XEROX CANADA

Debbie Pivnick, Director, Personnel staff

Xerox Canada
987 Yonge Street
Toronto, Ontario

Attention: Ms. S. Black
            Recruitment Manager

Dear Ms. Black:

Business Magazine describes your company as a dynamic leader in the field of office products. To maintain your leadership position, product pricing and customer service are paramount.

As an Analyst at Magna International, I developed pricing models for the launch of their most successful product to date, and welcome the opportunity to apply my skills and knowledge at Xerox Canada.

In my work experience and while earning my MBA through the part-time program, I have developed and demonstrated

- strong organization skills
- excellent communications and interpersonal skills
- problem-solving and analytical skills
- an ability to work effectively under pressure

I believe that my academic background, combined with my business experience, would allow me to quickly establish myself as a valuable contributor in your company, and look forward to a personal interview, at your earliest convenience.

Yours truly,

encl

Plant Manager

The "Spirit of Innovation" thrives at BASF Corporation where innovative thinking creates new products, new services and new worlds of technological excellence. BASF Corporation Chemicals Division, a driving force in the development/manufacture of industrial chemicals, is seeking an experienced Plant Manager for our Northeast U.S. chemical manufacturing plant.

The "hands-on" individual will be responsible for all manufacturing and associated support as well as plant safety. In addition, the successful candidate will act as liaison with our engineering group in new plant development.

Qualified applicants must possess:

- **BS in Chemical Engineering or Chemistry**
- **10 + years' experience in a chemical plant environment with 5 years in a leadership capacity (as Assistant Plant Manager or higher)**
- **Experience working with governmental agencies concerning environmental issues and compliances**

If you're committed to searching for breakthrough ideas, BASF is the place for you. In addition to competitive salaries and comprehensive benefits, there's a steadfast commitment to team spirit. For immediate consideration, please send your resume and salary requirements in confidence to: **Mr. Robert J. Moss, P.O. Box 152, Parsippany, NJ 07054.** An Equal Opportunity Employer.

The Spirit of Innovation

BASF Corporation
Chemicals Division

BASF

BASF CORPORATION
Gerald E. Albright, Director, Human Resources

Mr. Robert J. Moss
P. O. Box 152
Parsippany, NJ 07054

Dear Mr. Moss:

I'm contacting you regarding your *Plant Manager* opening. The fact that it is for BASF also heightened my interest. I believe you will be impressed by my capabilities as an Operations Executive whose leadership yields results. Since I'm presently employed, please treat this contact in confidence.

A regard for people is certainly a key to leadership, as well as a strategy of process control and purposeful commitment. This is my formula for meeting profit, quality, and delivery goals. I offer you a result-oriented professional who has combined technical training with management experience. For example:

CONTRIBUTIONS: RESULTS-ORIENTED

Please consider my record of contributions to other companies: (1) 50% improvement in yield of acceptable product to meet a 50% sales increase; (2) Managed a quality system highly regarded by the FDA that supported an increase in production output five-fold within 3 years with only a doubling of personnel.

EXPERIENCE: MANUFACTURING PROFESSIONAL

Please also consider my experience: (1) over 10 years progressive manufacturing experience; (2) associated with bulk chemicals, fermentation, sterile filling, tablets, aerosols; (3) involved in all phases of manufacturing plant operations, business, and technical.

TECHNICAL BACKGROUND: THEORY AND PRACTICE

And finally please consider my technical background: (1) MS in Chemistry and an MBA; (2) Data processing-plant business information; (4) Certified Quality Engineer—ASQC.

More than these credentials is the person. I strongly believe you will find a warm, friendly person with initiative, drive, and confidence. I look forward to our meeting personally.

Thanks for your time and consideration.

Sincerely,

MANAGER
Investor Relations

COMSAT Corporation, a high-tech and publicly traded telecommunications firm, is looking for a key individual to manage the Investor Relations program. This is an excellent opportunity to gain major visibility in a large firm.

This individual will interface with security analysts and shareholders; develop programs to enhance the value of COMSAT stock; and conduct financial and market analyses.

The qualified candidate will possess a college degree, a minimum of 5 years' financial or investment analysis experience, and strong interpersonal and communication skills.

In return, COMSAT provides highly competitive salaries, flexible benefits and continued opportunities for financial and management development. For prompt, confidential consideration, forward your résumé to: Staffing/MFK, COMSAT Corporation, 950 L'Enfant Plaza. S.W., Washington, DC 20024.

COMSAT
CORPORATION

COMSAT is an equal opportunity employer.

COMSAT
James C. Herger, Director, Human Resources

COMSAT Corporation
Staffing/MFK
950 L'Enfant Plaza, S.W.
Washington, D. C. 20024

Dear COMSAT Corporation:

I am responding to the employment opportunity listed in the March 1, 1990 edition of the Washington Post regarding the Manager, Investor Relations position.

I have six and one-half years of investor relations experience with a reputable Fortune 100 company. While at Procter and Gamble, I have had the opportunity to work extensively with Wall Street analysts, corporate shareholders, and senior management in developing aggressive and strategic investment programs to improve and enhance the value of our stocks and investments.

I believe that my experience with Procter & Gamble has prepared me for the challenge COMSAT has to offer. A brief summary of my qualifications includes:

- Well-developed skills in the areas of financial and investment analysis.

- Ability to successfully initiate and accomplish projects with high-quality results and minimal supervision.

- Continuous interaction with all levels of management.

- Excellent oral and written communication skills.

- MBA from Wharton Business School. Undergraduate degree in Marketing from Villanova University.

Thank you for considering my résumé and I look forward to meeting with you to discuss my interests and qualifications. I can be reached at 202/444-1000 during the day and 301/888-9000 in the evening.

Sincerely,

Enclosure

Marketing Representative

Shipboard and Ground Systems Group

Unprecedented opportunity and technical challenge. The resources and reach of a Fortune 50 leader in defense electronics. A proven reputation for excellence in advanced ship communications and navigation systems. All part of what Unisys can offer you.

As Marketing Representative, you will be the liaison with NAVSEA, OPNAV, NCSC and other laboratories as you work to identify new programs and collect data on customer intentions, requirements, funding and schedules. In this capacity, you'll have a key role in furthering our business in the areas of mine warfare, special warfare and amphibious warfare as well as marketing Foreign Military Sales (FMS) programs.

The successful candidate will have a BS in a technical discipline, 2 to 5 years marketing experience to the U.S. Navy and a thorough understanding of the U.S. Navy organization and the procurement process.

Find out more about the challenge, compensation and benefits that come with being on the Unisys team. Send your résumé in confidence to: Unisys Corporation, Shipboard and Ground Systems Group, Dept. WP0320CH, 12010 Sunrise Valley Drive, Reston, VA 22091. An equal opportunity employer.

Unisys Corporation
Wade T. Robinson, Director Planning and Staffing

Unisys Corporation
Shipboard & Ground Systems Group
Department WPO320CH
12010 Sunrise Valley Drive
Reston, VA 22091

Dear Employer:

The attached résumé is submitted in response to your April 24th advertisement in the Washington Post for a MARKETING REPRESENTATIVE. I have been hoping that your organization would be increasing its marketing force and I would be very interested in meeting with you to explain why I could add much to your marketing efforts.

As my résumé reflects, I have been successfully marketing to the U. S. Navy for four years. My primary products have been fire control systems and electronic warfare components. I have met and exceeded my marketing goal each of the four years and expanded my present employer's customer base in both domestic and foreign markets.

Of particular interest to you may be a point not addressed in my résumé. I have been recently invited to address two electronic warfare industry groups on my perception of where this marketplace is headed in the next five years. At one of those presentations I met Nancy Bergere, your Director, Navy Program Management. I am sure she could provide you some insight into my depth of understanding in the Navy Marketplace.

I would appreciate the opportunity to meet with you or your line management as soon as possible. I can be reached at my home telephone number in the evenings or discreetly through my office. I am willing to interview prior to or after normal working hours at your convenience.

I look forward to hearing from you soon. I will take the liberty of calling you if I have not heard from you by June 7.

Sincerely,

Enclosure

ASSOCIATE DIRECTOR FOR OPERATIONS

Beth Israel Medical Center offers an excellent opportunity
to a strong Healthcare Management Professional to join
our progressive and dynamic management team.

Reporting to the Vice President of Operations, you will
oversee a variety of clinical and support departments. Position requires 5-7 years of progressively responsible experience including at least 2 years at the Assistant Director
level. You must have leadership talent, strong communication and interpersonal skills, and a Master's degree in
Health Care Administration, Business or a related area.

We offer excellent salaries and benefits package. Please
send résumé with salary history to: S.R. (A), Human Resources Department.

BETH ISRAEL MEDICAL CENTER

First Avenue at East 16th Street
New York, NY 10003

An Equal Opportunity Employer
Committed to a SMOKE-FREE Environment

Beth Israel Medical Center

William A. Lockom, Senior Vice President, Human Resources

S. R. (A), Human Resources Department
First Avenue at East 16th Street
New York, NY 10003

Dear Sir:

In response to your advertisement in the February 28, 1990 issue of the <u>New York Times</u>, I would like to offer my candidacy for the position of Associate Director for Operations, in confidence. My current position on the hospital's senior executive management team, a Master's Degree in Healthcare Administration and extensive experience in acute care, community and university-affiliated teaching hospitals would allow me to be an asset to your management team and to your hospital.

The enclosed curriculum vitae reflects my highly visible position as an operations officer for the coordination of overall day-to-day hospital activities and the supervision of departmental activities as it relates to key departments and professional services. In this position, I am directly responsible for a $38 million annual operating budget.

My wide level of experience and accomplishments demonstrates the versatility and strong analytical and decision making abilities that are indigenous to the positions I have held. These skills, creativity, resourcefulness and the established ability to assume responsibility for developing solutions and their implementation characterize me as a professional problem solver. I also possess exceptional communication and interpersonal skills, which combined with strong leadership abilities, effectively respond to challenging positions. I am confident my skills and abilities warrant a high level position with broad responsibilities.

I would be pleased to discuss my background, career objectives, and business referrals with you and look forward to hearing from you shortly.

Sincerely,

Enc.

MANAGER, GENERAL ACCOUNTING

Regional financial services company headquartered in Birmingham, Alabama with over $2.7 billion in assets has an immediate opening for a Manager, General Accounting for the Corporate office. The successful candidate will possess a B. S. in Accounting, 3–5 years supervisory experience over general ledger, accounts payable, accounts receivable and the payroll function of an accounting office. Experience in budgeting, forecasting and Lotus spreadsheet a plus.

Secor Bank offers an excellent compensation and benefits package. Send résumé and salary requirement in confidence to:

Secor Bank
Attn: Pam Mills
1234 Ross Street
Birmingham, AL 35200

EOE M/F/H/V

Secor Bank
Executive Vice President, Human Resources

Ms. Pam Mills
Secor Bank
1234 Ross Street
Birmingham, AL 35200

Dear Ms. Mills:

I am applying for the General Accounting Manager position with Secor Bank which you advertised on December 1, 1989. While working for Associated Services, my current employer, I perform all the required functions that were described in your advertisement. I believe this experience, in conjunction with my strong academic background, has prepared me for the position of General Accounting Manager.

The enclosed résumé outlines in more detail my background and accomplishments in accounting. I look forward to hearing from you soon.

Sincerely,

Encl.

STAFF OFFICER FOR SPECIAL PROJECTS, Boston Public Library. Under executive direction serves in a liaison role with civic/cultural/educational agencies, city departments and media; takes part in projects developing an expanded base of donors; designs, develops, executes, evaluates or reports on special library projects. Assists in special assignments related to library planning, needs assessment, experimental services, library/community agency cooperation or development. Assists in development projects including donor relationships and preparation of public/private grant proposals. Prepares library reports and histories. Provides research in support of library planning. The successful candidate must have five years of appropriate library or related experience with three years at the managerial level; demonstrated ability to work with outside agencies and library staff; thorough knowledge and understanding of library history, objectives, and policies; initiative in planning and executing new studies and projects; experience in needs assessment and planning; demonstrated proficiency in writing and public speaking. Send resume to: John T. Barrett, Library Personnel Officer, Boston Public Library, 666 Boylston Street, Boston, MA 02117. An equal opportunity/affirmative action employer.

Boston Public Library

John Barrett, Library Personnel Officer

Mr. John T. Barrett
Library Personnel Officer
Boston Public Library
666 Boylston Street
Boston, MA 02117

Dear Mr. Barrett:

I was pleased to see Boston Public Library's advertisement in the September 15th edition of Library Hotline for the position of Staff Officer for Special Projects. As the enclosed resume indicates, my qualifications and interests make me an ideal candidate for this position.

For the past three years I have held the position of Director of Editorial Research and Co-ordination at the Carnegie Institute where it is my responsibility to oversee the planning, coordination and implementation of all grants requested from federal, state and private sources and to publicize through the local and national media all programs and services so funded. During fiscal year 1987-1988, under my direction, the Institute received a quarter of a million dollars in grant support; one third of this support was received from the private sector.

Prior to accepting the position at Carnegie, I held a number of management positions at the Billings Institute Library. The two most pertinent among these were: Media Relations Officer, 1984-1986, where I directed publicity and promotional strategies, coordinated the preparation/editing and distribution of flyers, press releases and news articles and arranged news conferences and media coverage for major events; Assistant Grants Writer, 1982-1984, where I assisted in identifying and developing possible Library programs for grant funding and wrote resulting grant proposals as well as the necessary interim and final reports for all projects funded. Our banner year, 1983, was the basis for the "Grantsmanship in a Library Setting" presentation I gave at the American Library Association Annual Conference in Dallas, Texas on July 2, 1985.

Because of the knowledge and skills I have acquired in the areas of interagency cooperation, donor relations and grantmanship through these and other positions I have held, I am confident that I will be an asset to the Boston Public Library.

Boston continues to hold a particular attraction for me since my undergraduate days at Boston University and I have been fortunate in being able to maintain my personal and professional contacts in the city through my written contributions to the Massachusetts Historical Review.

I will be in the Boston area during the month of October and am eager to learn more about the Staff Officer for Special Projects position and to discuss with you my qualifications for this position. You may reach me at (607) 362-4158 during the work day and at (607) 365-8305 during the evenings and on weekends to arrange for an interview. I look forward to hearing from you.

Sincerely,

Bibliography

Bly, Robert W., and Blake, Gary. *Dream Jobs.* New York: John Wiley & Sons, Inc., 1983.

An excellent guide for exploring nine careers that are challenging and fast-growing. Advertising, biotechnology, cable TV, computers, consulting, public relations, telecommunications, training and development, and travel. Covers what it takes, getting started, your first big break, terminology, and lots of resources.

Career Navigator. New York: Drake Beam Morin, Inc., 1987.

An excellent, comprehensive, easy-to-use computer-based job search system. Contains four disks for the IBM PC or compatible, a well-written handbook, and word processor. Provides hands-on assistance with quizzes, resources, and information for every aspect of the job search from identifying interests and values, to résumé writing, interview techniques, and negotiating and evaluating job offers. Helps create and print résumés and cover letters. Use with a letter quality printer.

Catalyst staff. *Marketing Yourself.* New York: Bantam Books, 1981.

Guide to résumés and interviews. Section on interviews is very effective. Interesting perspective chronicles both the interviewer and the interviewee's thoughts concerning the interview. Helpful tips.

Catalyst staff. *What to Do With the Rest of Your Life.* New York: Simon and Schuster, 1981.

Valuable guide to career options with lengthy essays on specific fields and career choices.

Hecklinger, Fred, and Curtin, Bernadette. *Training for Life.* Dubuque, Iowa: Kendall/Hunt, 1988.

A comprehensive resource for effective career and life planning. A workbook that will assist the reader in planning and achieving career and life-style goals.

Scheele, Adele. *Skills for Success.* New York: Ballantine Books, 1979.

Timeless guidelines and suggestions that will enable the reader to plan and achieve career satisfaction and success.

U. S. Department of Labor. *Occupational Outlook Handbook.* Washington, D.C.: Government Printing Office, 1989.

Excellent guide to 1988–1989 careers: pros, cons, and salary ranges. Organized by professions.

Wood, Patricia. *The 171 Reference Book.* Washington, D.C.: Workbooks, Inc., 1984.

The best available reference for completing an effective and competitive Standard Form (SF)-171.